Credits

Footprint credits
Editor: Nicola Gibbs
Production and layout: Emma Bryers
Maps: Kevin Feeney
Cover: Pepi Bluck

Publisher: Patrick Dawson
Managing Editor: Felicity Laughton
Advertising: Elizabeth Taylor
Sales and marketing: Kirsty Holmes

Photography credits
Front cover: StevePleydell/Shutterstock.com
Back cover: Rtimages/Shutterstock.com

Printed in Great Britain by CPI Antony Rowe, Chippenham, Wiltshire

MIX
Paper from responsible sources
FSC® C013604

Publishing information
Footprint *Focus Pembrokeshire & Gower*
1st edition

April 2013

ISBN: 978 1 909268 27 2
CIP DATA: A catalogue record for this book is available from the British Library

Published by Footprint
6 Riverside Court
Lower Bristol Road
Bath BA2 3DZ, UK
T +44 (0)1225 469141
F +44 (0)1225 469461
footprinttravelguides.com

Distributed in the USA by Globe Pequot Press, Guilford, Connecticut

The content of Footprint *Focus Pembrokeshire & Gower* has been taken directly from Footprint's *Wales Handbook*, which was researched and written by Rebecca Ford.

Contents

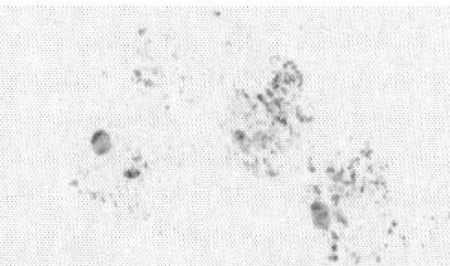

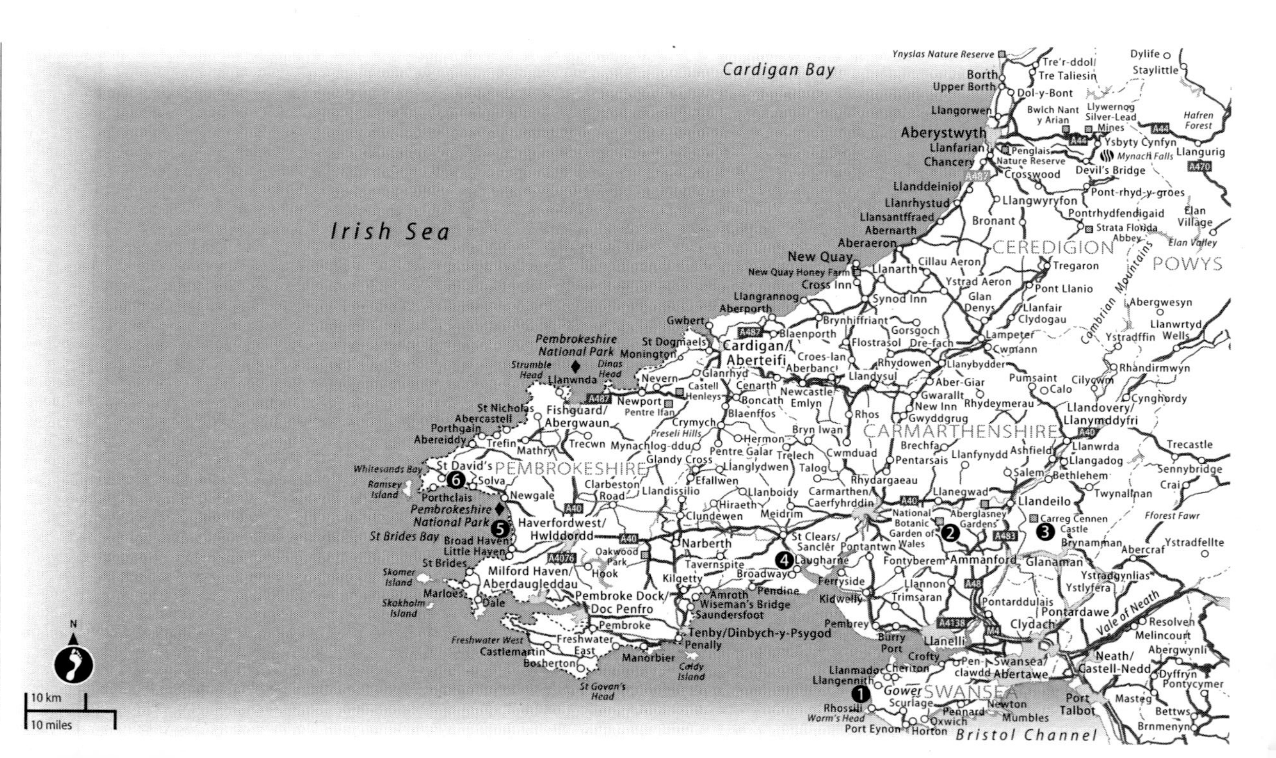

Cardigan Bay
Irish Sea
Bristol Channel
CEREDIGION
POWYS
CARMARTHENSHIRE
PEMBROKESHIRE
SWANSEA
Cambrian Mountains
Aberystwyth
New Quay
Aberaeron
Cardigan/
Aberteifi
Fishguard/
Abergwaun
St David's
Haverfordwest/
Hwlddordd
Milford Haven/
Aberdaugleddau
Pembroke Dock/
Doc Penfro
Pembroke
Tenby/Dinbych-y-Psygod
Narberth
Carmarthen/
Caerfyrddin
Llandeilo
Llandovery/
Llanymddyfri
Lampeter
Tregaron
Newport
St Clears/
Sanclêr
Laugharne
Kidwelly
Llanelli
Ammanford
Neath/
Castell-Nedd
Port Talbot
Swansea/
Abertawe
Mumbles
Gower
Rhossili
Worm's Head
Pembrokeshire
National Park
Strumble Head
Dinas Head
Preseli Hills
St Brides Bay
Whitesands Bay
Ramsey Island
Skomer Island
Skokholm Island
Caldy Island
St Govan's Head
National Botanic Garden of Wales
Aberglasney Gardens
Carreg Cennen Castle
Devil's Bridge
Ynyslas Nature Reserve
Elan Valley
Hafren Forest
Fforest Fawr
Vale of Neath
N
10 km
10 miles

Swansea, the second largest city in Wales and birthplace of the poet Dylan Thomas, has all the charm of a maritime hub – not to mention some excellent museums and a market that's well worth visiting for its seafood and Welsh specialities, such as laver bread. Next door, the Victorian seaside resort of Mumbles is popular with locals and visitors and has a fine array of pubs and restaurants. West of Swansea is the Gower Peninsula, Britain's first designated Area of Outstanding Natural Beauty and a mecca for surfers and lovers of soft, sandy beaches.

Further west, Carmarthenshire is a land of green hills, farms and ancient castles, extending out to the edge of the brooding Black Mountain. It's a quiet county full of history and mystery – the Romans mined gold here and legend has it that it's the birthplace of Merlin the magician. On its sleepy southern coast is Laugharne, where Dylan Thomas spent his final years.

Pembrokeshire is the most westerly county in Wales and one of the most beautiful. Its coastline of dramatic sea cliffs, glorious beaches and secluded coves has been attracting tourists for years – and its importance was recognized in 1952 when it was designated a national park. Punctuating this rugged coastline are pretty villages and seaside towns: on the south coast is the traditional – but far from tacky – bucket and spade resort of Tenby; on the north coast is the quietly comfortable little town of Newport. Far to the west is delightful St David's – Britain's smallest city and a spiritual centre since the sixth century. Today the best way to appreciate this unspoilt landscape is on foot; the Pembrokeshire Coast Path clings to the coastline as much as possible and provides some of the best walking in Britain.

Stretching northwards, the Ceredigion coast is a great place for wildlife lovers, and plenty of operators offer boat trips where you can spot dolphins, porpoises and seabirds.

Planning your trip

Best time to visit Pembrokeshire and the Gower

The high season runs from April until October, when most attractions are open and summer festivities are organized in almost every town and village. Summer evenings are long, while in winter it can get dark as early as 1600. School holidays (most of July and August) are the busiest time of year, when the most popular tourist destinations, such as the Pembrokeshire Coast, can get pretty packed. The best accommodation anywhere in the countryside must be booked well in advance for the summer months. That said, many of Wales' seaside hotspots are also best appreciated once the weather's turned nasty or even in clear winter sunlight.

Climate

The Welsh temperate climate is notoriously unpredictable. Bright, sunny mornings can turn into a downpour in the time it takes to butter your toast. Very generally, the mountains receive more rain than the coast and October to January are the wettest months. Winters can be pretty harsh, especially in the mountains, making hiking conditions treacherous. May to September are the warmest months (in particular July and August), but you can expect rain at any time of the year, even in high summer. So, you'll need to come prepared, and remember the old hikers' adage that there's no such thing as bad weather, only inadequate clothing.

Getting to Pembrokeshire and the Gower

Air

Cardiff has an international airport (see page 7) with flights from Scotland, Ireland and Europe. There are also daily flights from Amsterdam, from where it is possible to connect with airports all over the world. Otherwise, the main point of entry will be one of the English airports. Competition means it is usually cheapest to fly to one of London's five airports. Flights from North America arrive at Heathrow or Gatwick. Low-cost airlines generally fly into Gatwick, Stansted or Luton. Direct flights from Europe also arrive at Birmingham, Bristol, Liverpool and Manchester airports. Bristol Airport is most convenient for South Wales; Birmingham or Manchester airports are good for Mid and North Wales.

Flights from the rest of the UK and Ireland A small number of budget airlines fly daily to Cardiff International Airport from several British and Irish destinations. Prices on these flights can vary considerably, depending on the time and day of travel and how early you book your ticket. **Eastern Airways** ⓘ *www.easternairways.com*, flies direct from Birmingham, Newcastle and Aberdeen. **Flybe** ⓘ *www.flybe.com*, flies direct from Edinburgh, Glasgow and Belfast. **Aer Lingus** ⓘ *www.aerlingus.com*, flies direct from Dublin. Check the websites regularly to get the best deals.

Flights from continental Europe In addition to regular flights operated by the major national carriers, the surge in budget airline routes means that you can fly from practically

Don't miss…

1 **Gower Peninsula**, page 34.
2 **National Botanic Garden of Wales**, page 41.
3 **Carreg Cennen Castle**, page 42.
4 **Dylan Thomas Boathouse in Laugharne**, page 43.
5 **The Pembrokeshire Coastal Path**, page 46.
6 **St David's Cathedral**, page 50.

Numbers relate to the map on page 4.

anywhere in Europe to somewhere in Britain at cheap rates. Fares for a return ticket range from €15 to €300 on a scheduled flight. Budget airlines offer no frills: no meals, no reserved seating and baggage restrictions.

If you are flying direct to Cardiff, **Flybe** ⓘ *www.flybe.com*, flies from Paris; **Vuelling Airlines** ⓘ *www.vueling.com*, flies from Barcelona, Malaga and Alicante; **Thomson** ⓘ *www.thomson.co.uk*, flies from Faro; **KLM** ⓘ *www.klm.com*, flies from Amsterdam; and **Lufthansa** ⓘ *www.lufthansa.com*, flies from Dusseldorf.

Flights from North America There are no direct flights to Cardiff from North America, but journeys can be made via Amsterdam, from where there are frequent onward connections to Cardiff, taking just one hour 25 minutes. Alternatively, there are regular non-stop flights to London from many US and Canadian cities, including Atlanta, Boston, Calgary, Chicago, Dallas, Denver, Houston, Las Vegas, Los Angeles, Miami, Montreal, New York, Philadelphia, Phoenix, San Francisco, Seattle, Toronto, Vancouver and Washington DC, and many more connections to other cities. Non-stop flights are also available from **New York** to Manchester and Birmingham.

Flights from Australia and New Zealand There are no direct flights to Cardiff from Australia or New Zealand. The cheapest scheduled flights to London are via Asia with **Gulf Air** ⓘ *www.gulfair.com*, **Royal Brunei** ⓘ *www.bruneiair.com*, or **Thai Airways** ⓘ *www.thaiair.com*. Flights via Africa or North America are more expensive. The cheapest scheduled flights from New Zealand are with **Korean Air** ⓘ *www.koreanair.com*, **Thai Airways**, or **JAL** ⓘ *www.jal.com*, all of which fly via their home cities. The most direct route is via North America with **United Airlines** ⓘ *www.ual.com*, via Chicago or Los Angeles. **Emirates** ⓘ *www.emirates.com*, flies to Birmingham and Manchester from Sydney via Dubai, and Manchester is also served via Singapore on **Singapore Airlines** ⓘ *www.singaporeair.com*. Prices are slightly higher than flights to London.

Airport information

Arriving in Cardiff Cardiff International Airport (CWL) ⓘ *Rhoose, near Barry, T01446-711111, www.cwlfly.com*, Wales' small international airport, is 12 miles southwest of Cardiff's city centre and around a 30- to 40-minute taxi journey. The terminal's facilities include a few small bars selling drinks, snacks and teas and coffees, newsagents, a selection of duty free shops, and a children's play area. The airport is easily reached by car via the A4055, or taking the A4225 from the A48 or junction 33 off the M4. The taxi office is in the Arrivals hall and taxis can be prebooked on T01446-711747, approximately £25-30 to the city centre. Air buses operate regularly between the city's central train and main bus station and the airport, approximately costing £3.90.

Arriving in London **National Express** operates a frequent service between London's main airports. **London Heathrow Airport** ⓘ *16 miles west of London between junctions 3 and 4 on the M4, T0844-335 1801, www.heathrowairport.com*, is one of the world's busiest international airports and it has five terminals, so when leaving London, it's important to check which terminal to go to before setting out for the airport. To get into central London, the cheapest option is the London Underground Piccadilly Line (50 minutes). The fastest option is **Heathrow Express** ⓘ *T0845-6001515, www.heathrowexpress.com*, taking 15-20 minutes. There is a train service **Heathrow Connect** ⓘ *Heathrow, T0845-748 4950, www.heathrow connect.com*, which takes 25 minutes. Coaches to destinations all over the country are run by **National Express** ⓘ *T0871-781 8181, www.nationalexpress.com*. There are also buses to Reading for trains to Bristol and southwest England (www.railair.com).

London Gatwick Airport ⓘ *28 miles south of London, off junction 9 on the M23, T0844-892 03222, www.gatwickairport.com*, has two terminals, North and South, with all the usual facilities. To central London, there is the **Gatwick Express** ⓘ *T0845-850 1530, www.gatwickexpress.com, from £17.75 single online*, which takes 30 minutes. **Thameslink** rail services run from King's Cross, Farringdon, Blackfriars and London Bridge stations. Contact **National Rail Enquiries** ⓘ *T0845-748 4950, www.nationalrail.co.uk*, for further information. **EasyBus** (www.easybus.co.uk) is the cheapest option, with prices at £9.99 single, taking just over an hour. A taxi takes a similar time and costs from around £60.

London City Airport ⓘ *Royal Dock, 6 miles (15 mins' drive) east of the City of London, T020-7646 0000, www.londoncityairport.com*. Take the **Docklands Light Railway** (DLR) to Canning Town (seven minutes) for the **Jubilee line** or a connecting shuttle bus service. A taxi into central London will cost around £35.

London Luton Airport ⓘ *30 miles north of central London, 2 miles off the M1 at junction 10, southeast of Luton, Beds, T01582-405100, www.london-luton.co.uk*. Regular **First Capital Connect** trains run to central London; a free shuttle bus service operates between the airport terminal and the station. **Green Line** ⓘ *www.greenline.co.uk*, coaches run to central London, as does **easyBus** ⓘ *www.easybus.co.uk*. **National Express** ⓘ *www.nationalexpress.com*, operates coaches to many destinations. A taxi takes 50 minutes, costing from £70.

Stansted Airport ⓘ *35 miles northeast of London (near Cambridge) by junction 8 of the M11, T0844-335 1803, www.stanstedairport.com*. **Stansted Express** ⓘ *T0845-600 7245, www.stanstedexpress.com*, runs trains to London's Liverpool Street Station (45 minutes, £22.50 single). **EasyBus** ⓘ *www.easybus.co.uk, from £2*, **Terravision** ⓘ *www.terravision.eu, £9*, and **National Express** ⓘ *www.nationalexpress.com, from £8.50*, runsto central London (55 minutes to East London, one hour 30 minutes to Victoria). A taxi to central London takes around an hour to one hour 30 minutes, depending on traffic, and costs around £99.

Arriving at other UK airports **Bristol International Airport** (BRS) ⓘ *T0870-121 2747, www.bristolairport.co.uk*, eight miles south of the city centre, on the A38, has one terminal with standard facilities. A taxi to Bristol city centre costs £22, or the **Bristol International Flyer** coach links the airport with the railway station (Temple Meads) and the central bus station for onward connections, £11 return, 30 minutes.

Birmingham International Airport (BHX) ⓘ *T0121-767 5511, www.bhx.co.uk*, eight miles east of the city centre and has two terminals with standard facilities. A taxi to the centre costs around £25, or frequent trains run the 10-minute journey into the city centre. Connections to Wales can be made by rail or coach, with **National Express**, T08705-808080.

Liverpool John Lennon Airport (LPL) ⓘ *T0870-750 8484, www.liverpooljohnlennonairport.com*, is seven miles southeast of the city in Speke. A regular bus runs to Liverpool city centre, from where connecting buses and trains can be taken.

Manchester International Airport (MAN) ⓘ *T0161-489 3000, www.manchesterairport.co.uk*, south of the city centre, at Junction 5 of the M56. There are three terminals. Trains run from Manchester Piccadilly to North Wales. **National Express**, T08705-808080, runs from Terminals 1 and 2. A taxi into the city centre should cost around £20.

Newcastle International Airport (NCL) ⓘ *T0870-122 1488, www.newcastleairport.com*, is five miles north of the city. Metro trains run from the airport between 0545 and 2305, every 10 minutes, taking 20 minutes to the city centre or the central train station; single fare £2.10. **National Express** coaches also run from the airport.

Rail

There are fast and frequent rail services to Cardiff from London, Bristol, Birmingham and most other major cities. From London, trains leave from Paddington station for South Wales or from Euston station for Mid or North Wales. Trains from Birmingham, Manchester and London also head to Mid Wales (Machynlleth, Llandudno or Welshpool) and North Wales (Holyhead, Bangor, Llandudno, Porthmadog and Pwllheli); it may be necessary to change more than once. Ticket pricing is complicated (see page 11), but to get the best deal you should book in advance. Note that travel on Fridays or during the rush hour (before 1000 weekdays) is generally more expensive.

From continental Europe All international train connections pass through London. **Eurostar** ⓘ *T0990-186186, www.eurostar.com*, operates high-speed trains to London Waterloo from Paris (three hours) and Brussels (two hours 40 minutes) via Lille (two hours). There are substantial discounts for children (4-11 years) and for passengers who are under 26 years on the day of travel. It is worth keeping an eye open for special offers, especially in the low season. All other rail connections will involve some kind of ferry crossing (see below). For full details on rail services available, contact your national railway or **Rail Europe**, www.raileurope.com; they also provide information on routes, timetables, fares and discount passes.

Road

Bus/coach Road links to Wales are good and this is the cheapest form of travel. The main operator between England and Wales is **National Express** ⓘ *T08705-808080, www.nationalexpress.com*. Buses from London leave from Victoria station and travel via Bristol to South Wales (Newport, Cardiff, Swansea, Carmarthen and Pembroke Dock); via Birmingham and Shrewsbury to Mid Wales (Welshpool, Aberystwyth) or via Chester to North Wales (Wrexham, Llandudno, Bangor, Pwllheli and Holyhead). From the north of England, buses travel via Birmingham to South Wales, or via Manchester or Liverpool to North Wales, from where onward connections can be made. Tickets can be bought at bus stations or from a number of agents throughout the country. It's also worth checking **www.megabus.com** for cheaper, but slower, transport from London to Cardiff and Swansea.

Car The most direct way to reach South Wales by car from London and southern and western England is on the **M4** motorway. The M4 crosses the Severn Estuary via the dramatic Severn Bridge (£6.20 per car, toll payable westbound only – you can leave Wales for free!). To North Wales, the **A55** expressway runs all the way from Chester to Holyhead following the coast; or from the Midlands, the **A5** through Llangollen. Mid Wales is best reached by the **A495** from Shrewsbury to Welshpool and then the **A458**; or the **A456** from Birmingham.

From continental Europe If you're driving from continental Europe you can take the **Eurotunnel Shuttle Service** ⓘ *T0800-969992, www.eurotunnel.com*, a freight train which runs 24 hours a day, 365 days a year, and takes you and your car from Calais to Folkestone in 35-45 minutes. For bookings, call T08705-353535. Foot passengers cannot cross on the Shuttle. You can also take a cross-channel ferry, see below.

Sea

From Ireland There are direct ferry crossings from Ireland to Holyhead in North Wales and to Swansea, Fishguard and Pembroke Dock in the south. There are at least two sailings daily, apart from to Swansea which is served four times a week. There are more frequent sailings during summer. Fares vary considerably depending on the time of day, week and season. Check the websites for promotional offers; discounts are usually available for students and Hostelling International (HI) members.

Irish Ferries ⓘ *T0818-300400, www.irishferries.com*, runs ferries from Dublin to Holyhead (five daily, three hours 15 minutes) and Rosslare to Pembroke (two daily, three hours 45 minutes). Fast boats are also available.

Stena Line ⓘ *T01-204 7777 (Ireland), T08447-707070 (UK), www.stenaline.ie*, runs ferries from Dun Laoghaire and Dublin to Holyhead (two daily, one hour 45 minutes) and from Rosslare to Fishguard (two daily, 3½ hours).

From continental Europe There are ferries to England from many European ports; the most useful for access to Wales are **Harwich** (served by boats from Denmark, Germany and the Netherlands); **Dover** (served by boats from Belgium and France); and **Portsmouth** (served by boats from France and Spain). **Poole**, **Portsmouth** and **Plymouth** are also served by boats from France. Prices vary enormously according to season, check prices for specific dates on one of the many online booking agent websites: **www.cheapferry.com**, **www.ferry-to-france.co.uk**, **www.ferrycrossings-uk.co.uk** or **www.ferrysavers.com**, or by contacting major route operators direct: **P&O Ferries** ⓘ *T08716-642121, www.poferries.com*, run from France, Ireland, Belgium and Holland; and **Brittany Ferries** ⓘ *T0871-244 0744, www.brittany-ferries.com*, run from Spain and western France to Britain's south coast.

Paddle steamers During the summer months, the *Waverley* and the *Balmoral* paddle steamers travel from Penarth, Newport, Swansea and Porthcawl down the Bristol Channel to Ilfracombe in Devon and Minehead in Somerset. A one-way ticket costs around £15. This is a very pleasant and leisurely way to travel, however the cruises are cancelled during bad weather. Further information is available from **Waverley Excursions** ⓘ *T0845-130 4647, www.waverleyexcursions.co.uk*.

Transport in Pembrokeshire and the Gower

Compared to the rest of Western Europe, public transport in Britain is generally poor and can be expensive. Rail, in particular, can cost an arm and a leg, and is notoriously unreliable. Coach travel is cheaper but much slower. Some areas are poorly served by public transport of any kind, and if you plan to spend much time in rural areas, it may be worth hiring a car, especially if you are travelling as a couple or group. A useful website for all national public transport information is **Traveline** ⓘ *T0871-200 2233, www.traveline.info.*

Rail

The rail network in Wales is less extensive than the bus network and generally a more expensive way to travel. However, there are some wonderfully scenic journeys across the middle of the country and many heritage railways still exist (see box, page 12). Most trains operating within Wales are run by **Arriva Trains Wales** ⓘ *T08456-061660, www.arrivatrainswales.co.uk.*

Enquiries and booking **National Rail Enquiries** ⓘ *T08457-484950, www.nationalrail.co.uk*, are quick and courteous with information on rail services and fares but not always accurate, so double check. They can't book tickets but will provide you with the relevant telephone number. The website, www.thetrainline.co.uk, shows prices clearly.

Railcards There are a variety of railcards which give discounts on fares for certain groups. Cards are valid for one year and most are available from main stations. You need two passport photos and proof of age or status. A **Young Person's Railcard** is for those aged 16-25 or full-time students aged 26+ in the UK. It costs £28 for one year and gives a 33% discount on most train tickets and some other services (www.16-25railcard.co.uk). A **Senior Citizen's Railcard** is for those aged over 60, it is the same price and offers the same discounts as a Young Person's Railcard (www.senior-railcard.co.uk). A **Disabled Person's Railcard** costs £20 and gives a 33% discount to a disabled person and one other. Pick up an application form from stations and send it to Disabled Person's Railcard Office, PO Box 11631, Laurencekirk AB30 9AA. It may take up to 10 working days to be delivered, so apply in advance (www.disabledpersons-railcard.co.uk). A **Family & Friends Railcard** costs £28 and gives a 33% discount on most tickets for up to four adults travelling together, and 60% discount for up to four children (www.familyandfriends-railcard.co.uk). It's available to buy online as well as in most stations.

Within Wales, the **Explore Wales Pass** (www.arrivatrainswales.co.uk) allows you to travel on all mainline trains and almost all its buses for a specified period. The Explore Wales Pass allows four days rail travel and eight days bus travel taken in eight consecutive days £94, child £47. The **Explore South Wales** and the **Explore North and Mid Wales** passes each cost £64, child £32.

Road

Bicycle Wales, like the rest of Britain, is less cycle-friendly than some countries, but with plenty of rivers, valleys, mountains, coast and moorland to explore, cycling is a great way to get out and about into the heart of the Welsh countryside. You don't need to go mountain biking off-road to enjoy the peace and quiet of the area; there are plenty of rural backroads, especially unclassified roads and country lanes, which are not numbered but are signposted and marked on OS maps. The only problem with more remote areas is the scarcity of spare parts should something go wrong with your bike.

The rail thing

Wales is a great place for lovers of scenic railway journeys – the country is full of them. The railways were vital to the development of the country's industries in the 19th century and trains, hauled first by horses and then by steam, were used to transport goods such as coal and slate from mines and quarries (often set in inaccessible mountain regions) to ports where they could then be loaded onto ships and exported all over the world. It was in 1804 that the first steam locomotive travelled on iron rails, going along the Merthyr tramroad in south Wales. And the world's first passenger railway service was launched in Wales in 1807, taking people around Swansea Bay. When the industries declined so did the railways – and the final death knell for many were the beeching cuts of the 1960s, which axed lines throughout Britain, badly affecting rural areas of Wales. However, many old railway lines that were abandoned have been carefully restored by volunteers who now run vintage trains (usually steam) along the tracks. The best known scenic routes are in the north, but there are a few in the south of Wales too. Wales also boasts Britain's only mountain railway, which travels up Snowdon.

South Wales

Brecon Mountain Railway, Merthyr Tydfil, www.breconmountainrailway.co.uk

Mid Wales

Talyllyn Railway, Tywyn, www.talyllyn.co.uk
Vale of Rheidol Railway, Aberystwyth, www.rheidolrailway.co.uk
Welshpool & Llanfair Light Railway, Llanfair Caereinion, www.wllr.org.uk

North Wales

Bala Lake Railway, www.bala-lake-railway.co.uk
Ffestiniog Railway and **Welsh Highland Railway**, Porthmadog, www.festrail.co.uk
Llanberis Lake Railway, www.lake-railway.co.uk

Information on these services can be found at www.greatlittletrainsof wales.co.uk.

Other scenic railways include: **Fairbourne & Barmouth Steam Railway**, Fairbourne, www.fairbournerailway.com; **Gwili Railway**, near Carmarthen, www.gwili-railway.co.uk; **Llangollen Railway**, www.llangollen-railway.co.uk; **Snowdon Mountain Railway**, Llanberis, www.snowdonrailway.co.uk; and the **Teifi Valley Railway**, Cardigan, www.teifivalleyrailway.org.

There are also forest trails and dedicated routes along canal towpaths and disused railway tracks. These are part of the expanding National Cycle Network, which is covered by the *Official Guide to the National Network* (£9.99), published by the charity **SUSTRANS** ⓘ *T0117-929 0888, www.sustrans.co.uk*. There is also a series of demanding long-distance routes. The Wales Tourist Board provides good information at **www.cycling.visitwales.com**. The **Cyclists' Touring Club** (CTC) ⓘ *T01483-417217, www.ctc.org.uk*, the largest cycling organization in the UK, provides a wide range of services and information on transport, cycle hire and routes, from day rides to longer tours.

Transporting your bicycle You can cut down on the amount of pedalling you have to do by transporting your bike by train. Bikes can be taken free on most local rail services on a first come-first served basis, but only outside morning and evening rush hours (0730-0930 and 1600-1900). On long-distance routes you'll have to make a reservation at least

Pedal power

Wales offers some superb opportunities for cyclists, with everything from gentle circuits for families to challenging mountain bike trails for the adventurous (and fit) biker. You can cycle alongside canal towpaths, down quiet country lanes, beside lakes and reservoirs and along forest and mountain tracks.

The country has three long-distance trails that can be ridden over about a week:

The Lôn Las Cymru National Cycle Route (250 miles) runs north to south and takes you across the Snowdonia National Park and the Cambrian Mountains. It starts in Holyhead, Anglesey and cuts across the country to Cardiff or Chepstow.
The Celtic Trail (220 miles) goes from west to east, starting at Fishguard on the lovely Pembrokeshire coast and going across the country to Chepstow. It follows canal towpaths, disused railway tracks and quiet lanes.
The Lôn Cambrai Trail (113 miles) crosses Mid Wales, running between Shrewsbury on the border and Aberystwyth – where it links to the Lôn Teifi route (98 miles) which goes on to Fishguard.

Wales also boasts some of the finest mountain biking in the world. The best known tracks and bike bases are listed below.
Afan Forest Park, T01639-850564, www.afanforestpark.co.uk, southeast, near Neath, with four trails.
Brecon Beacons National Park, www.mtbbreconbeacons.co.uk, the active heart of Wales with 14 mountain bike routes, suitable for novices and the more experienced.
Coed y Brenin, T01341-440747, in North Wales, near Dolgellau, Wales' best-known mountain biking centre, with good facilities and an expanding network of trails.
Cwmcarn Forest, T01495-272001, www.cwmcarnforest.co.uk, in the southeast corner, half an hour from Cardiff and close to Newport, has the **Whyte Twrch Trail.**
Gwydyr Forest, www.forestry.gov.uk, in the north near Betws y Coed, has a long mountain trail.
Llanwrtyd Wells, Mid Wales, is a good base for exploring on a bike as it offers access to fine, unspoilt countryside and a variety of trails.
Machynlleth, Mid Wales, has three trails that start from the town centre and a purpose-built trail in the nearby **Dyfi Forest.**
Nant yr Arian, T01970-890453, in the northwest, near Aberystwyth, is set in the remote mountains, it has several trails including the challenging **Syfydrin Trail**.

These aren't the only places to cycle in the country though – there are cycle paths and trails everywhere. Just ask at local TICs and check out the following websites for loads more information on everything from maps, trail guides, bike repair shops and places to stay: www.mbwales.com for mountain biking; www.visitwales.co.uk for all sorts of cycling info; www.sustrans.org.uk for maps and general information.

24 hours in advance and pay a small charge. Space is limited on trains so it's a good idea to book as far in advance as possible. Bus and coach companies will not usually carry bikes, with the exception of national park bus services, such as the **Snowdon Sherpa**. Details are available on the CTC website.

Rental Bike rental is available at cycle shops in most large towns and cities and tourist centres. Expect to pay from around £20-30 per day, with discounts for longer periods, plus a refundable deposit. There are cycle shops and cycle hire companies in most large towns, and smaller towns and villages in popular tourist areas.

Bus and coach Travelling around Wales by bus is generally the cheapest form of public transport. Roads are well maintained and there are good bus links between towns and cities, but far less frequent in more remote rural areas. While it's possible to travel almost anywhere by bus, it can be slow-going and patience is required. There is a vast network of local and regional services throughout the country, including national parks. When travelling on local buses, try to have the right money as change is not always available.

Reservations A number of travel passes are available. Information on services throughout Wales is available from **Traveline Cymru** ⓘ *T0870-608208, www.traveline-cymru.org.uk*. Bus companies include: **Arriva Cymru** ⓘ *T08701-201088, www.arriva.co.uk*, serving north and west Wales; **First Cymru** ⓘ *T01792-582233, www.firstcymru.co.uk*, serving southwest Wales; **National Express** ⓘ *T08705-808080, www.nationalexpress.com*, serving major towns and cities throughout the country; and **Stagecoach** ⓘ *T01633-838856, www.stagecoachbus.com/south_wales*, serving southeast Wales.

Full-time students, those aged under 25 or over 60 or those registered disabled, can buy a **Coach Card** for £10 which is valid for one year and gets you a 30% discount on all fares. Children normally travel for half price, but with a **Family Card** costing £16, two children travel free with two adults. Available to overseas passport holders, the **Brit Xplorer Pass** offers unlimited travel on all National Express buses. Passes cost from £79 for seven days, £139 for 14 days and £219 for its month-long **Rolling Stone Pass**. They can be bought from major airports and bus terminals.

Car Travelling with your own transport is the ideal way to explore the country. This allows you the freedom to explore remote places in your own time. The main disadvantages are traffic congestion and parking, but this is only a problem in the main cities and on major roads, particularly at weekends and on bank holidays. Roads in Wales are generally a lot less busy than those in England, and driving is relatively stress-free, especially on the B-roads and minor roads.

Motoring organizations can help with route planning, traffic advice, insurance and breakdown cover. The two main ones are: the **Automobile Association (AA)** ⓘ *T0800-085 2721, emergency number T0800-887766, www.theaa.com*, which offers a year's breakdown cover starting at £38, and the **Royal Automobile Club (RAC)** ⓘ *T0844-273 4341, emergency number T08000-828282, www.rac.co.uk*, which has a year's breakdown cover starting at £31.99. Both have cover for emergency assistance. You can still call the emergency numbers if you're not a member, but you'll have to a pay a large fee.

Car hire Car hire is expensive and the minimum you can expect to pay is around £100 per week for a small car. Always check and compare conditions, such as mileage limitations, excess payable in the case of an accident, etc. Small, local hire companies often offer better deals than the larger multinationals. Most companies prefer payment with a credit card – some insist on it – otherwise you'll have to leave a large deposit (£100 or more). You need to have had a full driver's licence for at least a year and to be aged between 21 (25 for some companies) and 70.

Where to stay in Pembrokeshire and the Gower

Accommodation in Wales is plentiful, and the quality of what's available has improved greatly in recent years. Hotels range from world-class luxury, for which you can expect to pay at least £100 to over £250 a night, to dilapidated concerns with dodgy plumbing and threadbare carpets, though thankfully the latter have almost disappeared. For the privilege of staying at one of these less charming places you can still expect to pay £50-60 a night for a double room. Most of the more salubrious hotels, the ones that can afford to pay the cleaner but may not offer full room service, are likely to cost between £80-150 for a double room for a night. Generally it's still true to say that guests paying over £80 a night can expect a decent level of comfort and service: from well-sprung mattresses to fluffy bath towels and flowers in the room.

Hotels

Hotels range from top-notch country houses, with extensive grounds and sometimes spa facilities to smaller establishments like cosy inns. Wales also has an increasing number of boutique hotels which are small, classy and contemporary. You'll also find some restaurants with rooms – where accommodation tends to be good quality but simpler, as the emphasis is on the food – and inns, which are offering increasingly decent rooms.

At the lower end of the scale, there is often little to choose between cheaper hotels and guesthouses or B&Bs – in fact a good B&B can often be far better than a low-grade hotel, offering higher standards of comfort (and often cleanliness) and a more personal service. However, many small hotels are really just guesthouses, and are often family-run and every bit as friendly. Note that some hotels, especially in town centres or in fishing ports, may also be rather noisy, as the bar can often be the social hub. Rooms in most mid-range to expensive hotels almost always have bathrooms en suite. Many upmarket hotels offer excellent room-only deals in the low season. An efficient last-minute booking service is **www.laterooms.com**, which specializes in weekend breaks. Also note that many hotels offer cheaper rates for online booking through agencies such as **www.lastminute.com**. Some of the best accommodation is collected in the brochure by **Welsh Rarebits** ⓘ *T01570-470785, www.rarebits.co.uk.*

Guesthouses

Guesthouses occupy the middle ground between hotels and B&Bs. The quality of accommodation in guesthouses varies wildly: some provide exceptional value for the money in houses of great character; while others have seen much better days. They can usually charge anything from £50-100 for the night, occasionally quoting initially for half-board (dinner, bed and breakfast). Some have a restaurant, which may or may not be open to non-residents.

Guesthouses are often large, converted family homes with five or six rooms. They tend to be slightly more expensive than B&Bs, charging between around £35 and £55 per person per night. Although they are often less personal, they can provide better facilities, such as en suite bathrooms, TV in each room and private parking. In many instances they are more like small budget hotels. Many guesthouses offer evening meals, but this may have to be requested in advance. Information is available from the Wales Tourist Board, where you can book online at www.visitwales.co.uk. Some of the best small hotels, inns and guesthouses can be found in the brochure published by **Great Little Places** ⓘ *T01686-668030, www.wales.little-places.co.uk.*

Price codes

Where to stay

££££ over £160 **£££** £90-160

££ £50-90 **£** under £50

Prices include taxes and service charge, but not meals. They are based on a double room in high season.

Restaurants

£££ over £30 **££** £15-30 **£** under £15

Prices refer to the cost of a two-course meal, without a drink.

Bed and Breakfasts (B&Bs)

Bed & Breakfasts (B&Bs) provide the cheapest private accommodation. As their name suggests, they usually offer fairly straightforward accommodation in a private home, with a heart-stopping breakfast fry-up thrown in. Many are run by empty-nesters with beautiful period houses and gardens; elsewhere, the best of them tend to be on working farms. These days most have en suite or private bathrooms and TVs in the rooms – though do check beforehand to be sure. Again, their standards are extremely variable, but they're unlikely to cost much more than £80 per room per night, some as little as £50 – depending on their location as much as the quality they offer – and some hosts can really bring their area to life. Many hotels, guesthouses and B&Bs offer discounts for stays of more than one night, weekend deals, and high and low season prices. They can be booked through Tourist Information Centres (TICs). Some TICs charge a booking fee. Note that many B&Bs charge more than 50% of the room rate for single occupancy, so check beforehand.

Hostels

For those travelling on a tight budget, there is a large network of hostels offering cheap accommodation. These are also popular centres for backpackers and provide a great opportunity for meeting fellow travellers. Hostels have kitchen facilities for self-catering and some include a continental breakfast in the price or provide cheap breakfasts and evening meals. Advance booking is recommended at all times, and particularly from May to September and on public holidays.

In most major cities, national parks and other areas of outstanding natural beauty, budget accommodation can be found at **backpackers hostels** and **YMCAs**. Many campsites and youth hostels are run by the **Youth Hostel Association** ⓘ *Trevelyan House, Dimple Rd, Matlock, DE4 3YH, T0800-019 1700, T01629-592700, www.yha.org.uk*. A bed in a dormitory usually costs about £15 a night.

Self-catering

One of the most cost-effective ways to enjoy Wales is to hire a cottage with a group of friends or family. There are lots of different types of accommodation to choose from, to suit all budgets, ranging from high quality serviced apartments and luxury homes to windmills and lighthouse keeper's houses and basic cottages with few facilities.

The minimum stay is usually one week in the summer peak season, though many offer shorter stays of two, three or four nights, especially outside the peak season. Expect to pay at least £200 per week for a two-bedroom cottage in the winter, rising to £400-600 in the high season, or more if it's a particularly nice place.

Some TICs and a large number of private organizations keep lists of self-catering options on their books. Two of the more interesting are the **Landmark Trust** ⓘ *Shottisbrooke, Maidenhead, Berks, SL6 3SW, T01628-825925, www.landmarktrust.org.uk*, which rents out renovated historic landmark buildings, at a price; and the **National Trust** ⓘ *36 Queen Anne's Gate, London, SW1H 9AS, T0844-800 2070, brochure line T0844-800 2072, www.nationaltrustcottages.co.uk*, which provides a wide range of accommodation on its estates, from an old rectory to a gas-lit cottage.

Contacts

Coast and Country Holidays, T01239-881297, www.welsh-cottages.co.uk.
Menai Holiday Cottages, T01248-717135, www.menaiholidays.co.uk.
Nefyn Holidays, T01758-720674, www.nefynholidays.co.uk.
Snowdonia Tourist Services, T01766-513829, www.sts-holidays.co.uk.
Wales Holidays, T01686-628200, www.wales-holidays.co.uk.

Campsites

There are plenty of campsites around Wales. Many are geared towards caravans and vary greatly in quality and level of facilities – some have large, luxury static caravans and electricity, others are just fields on a farm. The most expensive sites, which charge up to £25 to pitch a tent, are usually well equipped. Sites are usually only open from April to October.

Campus accommodation

Several Welsh universities open their halls of residence to visitors during the summer vacation (late June to September). Many rooms are basic and small with shared bathrooms, but there are also more comfortable rooms with private bathrooms, twin and family units and self-contained apartments and shared houses. Bed and Breakfast, and self-catering options are all available. Prices for B&Bs tend to be roughly the same as most B&Bs, but self-catering can cost as little as £50 per person per week. Local tourist offices have information, or contact the **British Universities Accommodation Consortium** ⓘ *T0115-950 4571*, for a brochure. For Swansea contact T01792-295665, www.swan.ac.uk; and for Aberystwyth contact T01970-621960, www.aber.ac.uk.

Food and drink in Pembrokeshire and the Gower

Food

The quality of food in Wales has improved enormously in recent years. Since the 1980s the British in general have been shrugging off their reputation for over-boiled cabbage and watery beef and although the food revolution took a bit longer to reach Wales, the Welsh have now made determined efforts to improve the quality of food on offer. Annual awards are made to restaurants and pubs serving high-quality food, as well as to outstanding Welsh food producers. Although Wales has never had a cuisine that's particularly distinct to that of the rest of Britain, it does have some excellent local produce, such as lamb and fish, as well as a number of traditional native dishes. Organic produce is also widely available. Many chefs are now making the most of this, combining ingredients in imaginative ways, and creating lighter, fresher versions of traditional dishes to create what's generally known as 'modern Welsh' cuisine. An increasing number of contemporary restaurants, bistros and so-called 'gastropubs' (where the emphasis is on good food rather than boozing) are opening throughout the country. The cities also generally have Italian and Indian restaurants and most places, including pubs, will offer at least one choice for vegetarians. Not surprisingly, the capital Cardiff has the most cosmopolitan food culture and you can eat anything there, from Mexican to Japanese. You shouldn't go hungry in Wales as even the smallest places usually have a takeaway outlet, generally offering Chinese food, baked potatoes with fillings or, of course, fish and chips – which can be excellent if well cooked. The situation's not perfect and plenty of places still do fatty pies, greasy chips and overcooked veg but things are improving all the time.

So what should you look out for in Wales? Well, meat eaters can try Welsh **lamb** and Black **beef**, which have been farmed on the local pastures and hills for centuries. There is also salt marsh lamb, which is raised on coastal areas feeding on saline rich vegetation which gives it a distinctive, delicate flavour. Lamb is used to make *cawl*, a traditional broth made with leeks, potatoes and other veg.

Then there's a wide range of **seafood**, perhaps the best known of which are the Penclawdd cockles which are collected on the Gower Peninsula and sold at Swansea market. You'll also find oysters from Pembroke and Anglesey, crabs and lobsters from places like Milford Haven, and other delicacies like scallops and clams. The coastline, as well as Wales' lakes and rivers, mean that lots of fresh **fish** is available, from salmon to less familiar Arctic char and *sewin* (sea trout). The shore also gives Wales one of its most distinctive native dishes – **laver bread** (*bara lawr*). This is a sort of lettuce-like seaweed that is mixed with oatmeal and generally fried and eaten for breakfast with bacon – it's a Swansea favourite.

Lots of **vegetables** in Wales are produced organically – look out for the famous Welsh leek, often combined with potatoes in soups and stews. Then there are some wonderful Welsh **cheeses** varying from the famous Caerphilly, which is mild, white and crumbly to Llanboidy, a smooth, hard cheese. Most of the cheese-making production is in West Wales, especially the Teifi and Towy valleys. There are some delicious soft goat's cheeses available too. Hard cheeses are often flavoured with other ingredients such as laverbread, chives or garlic to create more intense flavours. Cheese, of course, features in some of Wales' native dishes such as **Welsh rarebit**, essentially cheese mixed with beer (or sometimes Worcester sauce) and grilled on toast, and **Glamorgan sausages**, made from cheese, herbs and vegetables.

Traditional Welsh baking recipes are simple but flavoursome. In tea rooms you might see **bara brith** (speckled bread), which is a sort of dried fruit loaf made with tea, and

Welsh cakes, which are made with fruit and cooked on a griddle. Welsh producers are also making **ice cream**, sometimes flavoured with local honey, yoghurts, preserves and handmade chocolates. Keep an eye out for them in delis and markets.

Eating out

For a cheap meal, your best bet is a pub, hotel bar or café, where you can have a one-course meal for around £7, though don't expect gourmet food. The best value is often at lunch time, when many restaurants offer three-course set lunches or business lunches for less than £15. You'll need a pretty huge appetite to feel like eating a three-course lunch after your gigantic cooked breakfast, however. Also good value are the pre-theatre dinners offered by many restaurants in the larger towns and cities (you don't need to have a theatre ticket to take advantage). These are usually available from around 1730-1800 till 1900-1930. The biggest problem with eating out in the UK is the limited serving hours in many pubs and hotels outside the main cities. These places often only serve food between 1230 and 1400 and 1700 and 1900, seemingly ignorant of the eating habits of foreign visitors, or those who would prefer a bit more flexibility during their holiday. In small places especially it can be difficult finding food outside these times. Check out www.uk-food-drink-travel.com for more information.

Drink

Drinking is taken as seriously in Wales as the rest of Britain and **beer** (flat, brown and made with hops) is still the national drink – although it faces serious competition from continental lagers and alcopops. **Real ale**, made from small independent breweries, is available in many pubs in Wales. Pubs are still the traditional places to enjoy a drink: the best are usually 'freehouses' (not tied to a brewery) and feature log fires in winter, pretty gardens for the summer, and thriving local custom. Those that also have accommodation are known as 'inns', while more and more are offering good food. The local brews are Brains beer, which is made in Cardiff and ale made at the Felinfoel brewery near Llanelli. As well as widely available 'bitter' you'll also find 'dark' in Wales, a sweeter, darker coloured beer.

Welsh **wines** are also now produced in the south, while the most recent additions to the local drinks industry are distilled drinks made in Penderyn near the Brecon Beacons. There's Penderyn Welsh **whisky**, Brecon gin, vodka and a creamy liqueur, www.welsh-whisky.co.uk. Pubs are usually open from around 1100-2230 or 2300 Monday to Saturday, and on Sunday from around 1200-1500 and 1800-2230, though those in bigger cities might open for longer.

The eisteddfod

Meaning a 'meeting of bards' or 'a gathering' the eisteddfod (plural eisteddfodau) is a uniquely Welsh event. Its origins stretch far back in history to the days when poets, singers and musicians would gather to compete for positions in the households of the gentry. The first major eisteddfod was held in 1176 in Cardigan Castle and after that they were held regularly, until the practice began to die out in the 17th and 18th centuries. They were revived in the 19th century, the first modern one taking place at Carmarthen. Now they take place all over Wales, with two major annual festivals – the International Musical Eisteddfod (www.international-eisteddfod.co.uk) and the Royal National Eisteddfod. The latter alternates between locations in north and south Wales and involves ceremonies in which prizes are awarded for poetry, prose, and music. Proceedings are conducted in Welsh and it's a fascinating insight into the country and its traditions. Visitors come from all over the world. The 2013 Royal National Eisteddfod will be held from 2-10 August in Denbighshire. The 2014 event will run from 1-9 August in Llanelli. Further details at www.eisteddfod.org.uk.

Festivals in Pembrokeshire and the Gower

Details are provided in the listings for each area. Also check www.cerddystwyth.co.uk.

Jan Hen Galen (13 Jan). Celebration of 'Old New Year' according to the Julian calendar in the Gwaun Valley, Pembrokeshire.

Mar St David's Day. Celebrations throughout Wales, on 1 Mar.

May St David's Cathedral Festival, www.stdavids cathedral.org.uk. Classical concerts at St David's Cathedral.

May Pembrokeshire Folk Festival, www.pembrokeshire-folk-music.co.uk.

May-Sep Swansea Bay Festival, www.swanseabayfestival.co.uk. Various events throughout the summer including an outdoor cinema.

Jun Gower Folk Festival, www.halfpenny folkclub.com. Music fest held in Swansea.

Jun Dragon Festival, www.newcastle-emlyn.com/dragon-festival. Newcastle Emelyn, Carmarthenshire.

Jun Pembrokeshire Fish Week, www.pembrokeshirefishweek.co.uk.

Jun Wales National Air Show, www.wales nationalairshow.com. Takes place in Swansea Bay and features the Red Arrows.

Jun/Jul Dinefwr Literature Festival, www.dinefwrliteraturefestival.co.uk.

Jul Llandeilo Festival of Music, www.llandeilomusicfestival.org.uk.

Sep Swansea Festival of Music and the Arts, www.swanseafestival.co.uk. Opera, ballet, drama and music, late Sep and early Oct.

Sep Tenby Arts Festival, www.tenbyarts fest.co.uk. Lively performances, talks and art in seaside town of Tenby.

Nov Dylan Thomas Festival, Swansea, www.dylan thomas.org. Events and readings celebrating the life and works of the national poet.

Public holidays

New Year's Day (1 Jan); **Good Friday** and **Easter Monday**; **May Day Bank Holiday** (the first Mon in May); **Spring Bank Holiday** (the last Mon in May); **Summer Bank Holiday** (the last Mon in Aug); **Christmas Day** (25 Dec) and **Boxing Day** (26 Dec). There are also local public holidays in spring and autumn. Dates vary from place to place. Banks are closed during these holidays, and sights and shops may be affected to varying degrees. Contact the relevant Area Tourist Board for more details.

Essentials A-Z

Accident and emergency

For police, fire brigade, ambulance and, in certain areas, mountain rescue or coastguard, T999 or T112.

Disabled travellers

Wheelchair users, and blind or partially sighted people are automatically given 34-50% discount on train fares, and those with other disabilities are eligible for the **Disabled Person's Railcard**, www.disabledpersonsrailcard.co.uk, which costs £20 per year and gives a third off most tickets. If you will need assistance at a railway station, call the train company that manages the station you're starting your journey from 24 hrs in advance. Disabled UK residents can apply to their local councils for a concessionary bus pass. **National Express** has a helpline for disabled passengers, T08717-818179, to plan journeys and arrange assistance. They also sell a discount coach card for £10 for people with disabilities.

Useful organizations include:

Disability Wales, T02920-887325, www.disabilitywales.org. The national association of disability groups in Wales.

Radar, T020-7250 3222, www.radar.org.uk. A good source of advice and information. It produces an annual National Key Scheme Guide and key for gaining access to over 9000 toilet facilities across the UK.

Tourism for all, T0845-124 9971, www.holidaycare.org.uk, www.tourismforall.org.uk. An excellent source of information about travel and for identifying accessible accommodation in the UK.

Electricity

The current in Britain is 240V AC. Plugs have 3 square pins and adaptors are widely available.

Health

For minor accidents go to the nearest casualty department or an Accident and Emergency (A&E) Unit at a hospital. For other enquiries phone NHS Direct 24 hrs (T0845-4647) or visit an NHS walk-in centre. See also individual town and city directories throughout the book for details of local medical services.

Language

Wales is officially bilingual and as soon as you enter the country you will be aware of this, with road signs and place names appearing in both Welsh and English. *Cymraeg*, as the language is known in Welsh, is spoken by around 500,000 people and is closely related to other Celtic languages like Breton and Cornish. The language has its heartlands in the north and west, particularly in places like Anglesey, the Llŷn Peninsula, Caernarfon and parts of Cardiganshire and Carmarthenshire; you're less likely to hear it in the capital Cardiff or in towns and villages along the border. For many people it is their mother tongue and you will have plenty of opportunities to hear this ancient language (probably the oldest in Europe) spoken. The language has received plenty of support, unlike Cornish which has been shamefully neglected. There is a Welsh language television station S4C (Sianel Pedwar Cymru): established in 1982 it broadcasts for several hours in Welsh each day. Shows include the long running BBC Welsh soap *Pobol y Cwm* or 'People of the Valley', set in the fictional village of Cwmderi. The digital S4C2 channel shows the proceedings of the Welsh Assembly, and viewers can choose to watch in English or Welsh. Welsh language radio includes the BBC's Radio Cymru and a number of commercial stations such as Radio Ceredigion, which is bilingual. More information on the BBC services at www.bbc.co.uk/cymru.

Welsh language courses

There are several websites with information on summer courses and evening classes in Welsh, such as www.acen.co.uk and www.coleg.powys.ac.uk. There are also academic courses, www.cs.cf.ac.uk, and summer courses in Glamorgan, www.welshforadults.cardiff.ac.uk.

Cardiff Language Academy, Oliver House, 16/17 High St, Cardiff, T02920-226047, www.cmla.uk.com.

Ceredigion Language Centre, T01545-572713, www.ceredigion.gov.uk.

Welsh Language Society, T01970-624501, www.cymdeithas.com. Based in Aberystwyth.

Money → *For up-to-date exhange rates, see www.xe.com.*

The British currency is the pound sterling (£), divided into 100 pence (p). Coins come in denominations of 1p, 2p, 5p, 10p, 20p, 50p, £1 and £2. Banknotes come in denominations of £5, £10, £20 and £50. The last of these notes are not widely used and may be difficult to change.

Banks and bureaux de change

Banks tend to offer similar exchange rates and are usually the best places to change money and cheques. Outside banking hours you'll have to use a bureau de change, which can be easily found at the airports and train stations and in larger cities. Thomas Cook and other major travel agents also operate bureaux de change with reasonable rates. Avoid changing money or cheques in hotels, as the rates are usually poor. Main post offices and branches of Marks and Spencer will change cash without charging commission.

Cost of travelling

Wales can be an expensive place to visit. There is budget accommodation available, however, and backpackers will be able to keep their costs down. Fuel is a major expense and won't just cost an arm and a leg but also the limbs of all remaining family members, and public transport – particularly rail travel if not booked in advance – can also be pricey, especially for families. Accommodation and restaurant prices also tend to be higher in more popular destinations and during the busy summer months.

The minimum daily budget required, if you're staying in hostels or camping, cycling or hitching (not recommended), and cooking your own meals, will be around £30 per person per day. If you start using public transport and eating out occasionally that will rise to around £35-40. Those staying in slightly more upmarket B&Bs or guesthouses, eating out every evening at pubs or modest restaurants and visiting tourist attractions can expect to pay around £60 per day. If you also want to hire a car and eat well, then costs will rise considerably to at least £75-80 per person per day. Single travellers will have to pay more than half the cost of a double room, and should budget on spending around 60-70% of what a couple would spend.

Credit cards and ATMs

Most hotels, shops and restaurants accept the major credit cards though some places may charge for using them. Some smaller establishments such as B&Bs may only accept cash.

Currency cards

If you don't want to carry lots of cash, prepaid currency cards allow you to preload money from your bank account, fixed at the day's exchange rate. They look like a credit or debit card and are issued by specialist money changing companies, such as Travelex and Caxton FX. You can top up and check your balance by phone, online and sometimes by text.

Money transfers

If you need money urgently, the quickest way to have it sent to you is to have it wired to the nearest bank via Western Union,

T0800-833 833, www.westernunion.co.uk, or **MoneyGram**, www.moneygram.com. The Post Office can also arrange a MoneyGram transfer. Charges are on a sliding scale; so it will cost proportionately less to wire out more money. Money can also be wired by **Thomas Cook**, www.thomasexchangeglobal.co.uk, or transferred via a bank draft, but this can take up to a week.

Opening hours

Businesses are usually open Mon-Sat 0900-1700. In towns and cities, as well as villages in holiday areas, many shops open on a Sun but they will open later and close earlier. For banks, see above. For TIC opening hours, see the tourist information sections in the relevant cities, towns and villages in the text.

Post

Most post offices are open Mon-Fri 0900 to 1730 and Sat 0900-1230 or 1300. Smaller sub-post offices are closed for an hour at lunch (1300-1400) and many of them operate out of a shop. Stamps can be bought at post offices, but also from many shops. A 1st-class letter weighing up to 100 g to anywhere in the UK costs 60p (a large letter over 240 mm by 165 mm is 90p) and should arrive the following day, while 2nd-class letters weighing up to 100 g cost 50p (69p) and take between 2-4 days. For more information about Royal Mail postal services, call T08457-740740, or visit www.royalmail.com.

Safety

Generally speaking, Wales is a safe place to visit. English cities have their fair share of crime, but much of it is drug-related and confined to the more deprived peripheral areas. Trust your instincts, and if in doubt, take a taxi.

Taxes

Most goods are subject to a Value Added Tax (VAT) of 20%, with the major exception of food and books. VAT is usually already included in the advertised price of goods. Visitors from non-EU countries can save money through shopping at places that offer Tax Free Shopping (also known as the Retail Export Scheme), which allows a refund of VAT on goods that will be taken out of the country. Note that not all shops participate in the scheme and that VAT cannot be reclaimed on hotel bills or other services.

Telephone → *Country code +44.*

Useful numbers: operator T100; international operator T155; directory enquiries T192; overseas directory enquiries T153.

Most public payphones are operated by **British Telecom** (BT) and can be found in towns and cities, though less so in rural areas. Numbers of public phone booths have declined in recent years due to the advent of the mobile phone, so don't rely on being able to find a payphone wherever you go. Calls from BT payphones cost a minimum of 60p, for which you get 30 mins for a local or national call. Calls to non-geographic numbers (eg 0845), mobile phones and others may cost more. Payphones (few and far between these days) take either coins (10p, 20p, 50p and £1), 50c, 1 or 2 euro coins, credit cards or BT Chargecards, which are available at newsagents and post offices displaying the BT logo. These cards come in denominations of £2, £3, £5 and £10. Some payphones also have facilities for internet, text messaging and emailing.

For most countries (including Europe, USA and Canada) calls are cheapest Mon-Fri between 1800 and 0800 and all day Sat-Sun. For Australia and New Zealand it's cheapest to call from 1430-1930 and from 2400-0700 every day. However, the cheapest ways to call abroad from Wales is not via a standard UK landline provider. Calls are free using **Skype** on the internet, or you can route calls from your phone through the internet with **JaJah** (www.jajah.com) or from a mobile using **Rebtel**. Many phone companies offer discounted call rates by calling their access number prior to dialling the number you want, including www.dialabroad.co.uk and www.simply-call.com.

Area codes are not needed if calling from within the same area. Any number prefixed by 0800 or 0500 is free to the caller; 08457 numbers are charged at local rates and 08705 numbers at the national rate.

Time

Greenwich Mean Time (GMT) is used from late Oct to late Mar, after which time the clocks go forward 1 hr to British Summer Time (BST).

Tipping

Tipping in Wales is at the customer's discretion. In a restaurant it is customary to leave a tip of 10-15% if you are satisfied with the service. If the bill already includes a service charge, which is likely if you are in a large group, you needn't add a further tip. Tipping is not normal in pubs or bars. Taxi drivers may expect a tip for longer journeys, usually around 10%.

Tourist information

Tourist Information Centres (TICs)

Most cities and towns that you're likely to visit in Wales will have a local Tourist Information Centre (TIC), which can give you information on local attractions, restaurants and accommodation (including handling bookings – for a small fee) and help with visitors' enquiries, such as where to find an internet café. Many sell books, local guides, maps and souvenirs, and some have free street plans and leaflets describing local walks. In general, tourist offices tend to cater to those interested in taking tours or day trips, and are less useful if you're on a tight budget, in which case youth hostels can provide much the same information. See individual town information sections for lists of local TICs.

Museums, art galleries and stately homes

The **National Trust**, T0844-800 1895, www.nationaltrust.org.uk, plays an active role in protecting and managing stately homes, gardens and the countryside of Wales and owns 133 miles of the Welsh coastline. If you're going to be visiting several sights during your stay, then it's worth taking annual membership or investing in a National Trust Touring Pass, available for 7 or 14 days.

A similar organization is **CADW**, www.cadw.wales.gov.uk, the historic environment agency responsible for protecting and conserving Wales' historic buildings, parks, monuments, gardens, landscapes and underwater archaeology. *Cadw* (pronounced *cad-oo*) is a Welsh word meaning 'to keep'. If you're planning to visit a number of places, it may be worth buying a CADW Explorer Pass: 3-day pass £13.20, 2 adults £20.30, family £28; 7-day pass £19.85, 2 adults £31.60, family £38.75.

Finding out more

A good way to find out more before your trip is to contact **Visit Britain**, which represents **Visit Wales** abroad. Their website, www.visitbritain.com, is very useful as a first-stop directory for accommodation. Alternatively, you can write to the head office at Brunel House, 2 Fitzalan Rd, Cardiff, CF24 4QZ. Both organizations provide a wealth of free literature and information such as maps, city guides, events calendars and accommodation brochures. Travellers with special needs should also contact their nearest Visit Britain office (see below). For more detailed information on a particular area, contact the area tourist boards. **Tourist Information Centres** (TICs) exist in most Welsh towns and **National Park Information Centres** area good source of information for outdoor activities such as walking. Details are provided in the Ins and Outs section at the beginning of each area.

The Countryside Code

1 Drive carefully and behave courteously to other motorists and cyclists on narrow, winding roads. Park vehicles where they will not be a hazard or disruption to other motorists, residents or businesses.
2 Keep to public paths through farmland to minimize crop damage and avoid 'short-cuts' on steep terrain to prevent soil erosion and damage to vegetation.
3 Litter is an eye-sore, harmful to farm animals, wildlife and the water supply. Leave no waste and take all your rubbish home.
4 Protect wildlife, plants and trees.
5 Respect ancient monuments, buildings and sites of religious importance. Do not vandalize or cause graffiti.
6 Avoid damaging crops, walls, fences and farm equipment; leave all gates as you find them.
7 Do not collect wild flowers, seabird eggs or historical artefacts.
8 Avoid pollution of the water supplies – there are few toilets outside of villages so when walking in the countryside bury human waste and toilet paper in the ground and at least 30 m from water courses.
9 Guard against risk of fire from matches, cigarettes, stoves and campfires.
10 Keep dogs under control, especially when near to sheep at lambing-time, seabird nesting sites at cliff edges. Avoid dog-fouling in public places.
11 Respect the peace, solitude and tranquillity of the countryside for others to enjoy – keep noise to a minimum.
12 The landscape can be spectacular but dangerous – take particular care along precipitous cliff edges, hilltops and slippery coastal paths.
13 Stay away from working areas on the moors and hills during game shooting, lambing season, deer culling and heather burning, and respect other locally or nationally imposed access restrictions.
14 Report any damage or environmental concerns to the landowner or Natural Resources Wales, T0300-065 3000. or the Environment Agency's incident hotline T0800-807060 (Freephone, 24-hour service), www.environment-agency.gov.uk.
15 Be adequately prepared when you walk in the hills – check the weather forecast, carry warm, waterproof clothing and adequate food and water supplies, and know how to use a map and compass.

Useful websites

The official Welsh Tourist Board site and the various area tourist board sites have information on accommodation, transport and tourist sites as well as outdoor activities such as walking, skiing and fishing. Other useful websites include:

Travel and leisure

www.aboutbritain.com Useful links for accommodation and travel.
www.aboutwales.co.uk An encyclopaedia of information about Wales.
www.britannia.com A huge UK travel site. Click on 'Wales guide' for a massive selection of subjects plus links to various sites including newspapers.
www.bbc.co.uk The UK's most popular site with an excellent what's on guide.
www.data-wales.co.uk A wealth of facts and information on everything from festivals to pronunciation of Welsh names.
www.whatsonwhen.com Has a huge range of upcoming events around the world.
www.uktrail.com Provides comprehensive information on transport and hostels.
www.visitbritain.com Practical informative site with useful links and ideas.

Walking in Wales

The Wales Coast Path (www.walescoastpath.gov.uk) opened in 2012 and is the country's newest long-distance path. It is 870 miles long and runs from the mouth of the River Dee in North Wales right around the coast to Chepstow in the south.

Beacons Way stretches 98 miles across the Brecon Beacons National Park, from Holy Mountain (north of Abergavenny) to Bethlehem in the west. It can be split into sections over 8-10 days and is a great way of exploring the wilder reaches of the area. Further details on www.ldwa.org.uk

Cambrian Way (www.cambrianway.org.uk), 274 miles, the longest and toughest path from Cardiff to Conwy via Snowdon. Guidebook by Tony Drake, available from the Ramblers' Association.

Coed Morgannwg Way, 36 miles, in the Valleys follows forest tracks from Gethin Woodland Park near Merthyr Tydfil, to Margam, near Neath. Guide published by Neath and Port Talbot County Borough Council.

Dyfi Valley Way, 102 miles, goes from Aberdovey and takes in the site of King Arthur's last battle, Camlan.

Glyndwr's Way (www.nationaltrail.co.uk), 135 miles, National Trail, starts in Knighton, on the border and runs through Llandiloes, on to Machynlleth, then back through Llanwddyn and on to Welshpool.

Landsker Borderlands Trail, 60 miles, circular walk in Pembrokeshire, start/finish Canaston Bridge.

Llyn Peninsula (Edge of Wales) Walk, 84 miles around the Llyn coast, starting in Caenarfon and finishing in Porthmadog

Monnow Valley Walk, 37 miles, Hay-on-Wye to Monmouth.

The North Wales Path stretches 60 miles and connects Prestatyn and Bangor.

Offa's Dyke Path (www.nationaltrail.co.uk/OffasDyke), 177 miles, follows, as far as possible, the line of Offa's Dyke from Prestatyn to Chepstow, meandering along the border of England and Wales. It runs through Knighton and passes very close to Montgomery and Welshpool.

The Pembrokeshire Coast Path (www.pcnpa.org.uk), 186 miles, is a waymarked National Trail that runs around the coast from St Dogmaels near Cardigan to Amroth near Tenby.

The Severn Way (www.severnway.com), 224 miles, traces the course of the River Severn from its source on Plynlimon to the Bristol Channel; 55 miles of the route are in Powys.

Three Castles Walk, 20 mile circuit, links castles at Grosmont, Skenfrith and White Castle. Guidebook from Monmouthshire County Council.

Wye Valley Walk (www.wyevalleywalk.org), 136 miles, from Chepstow to Plynlimon in Powys. The walk takes you through some lovely pastoral landscapes – including that round Tintern Abbey – and passes several market towns, such as Monmouth, Ross-on-Wye and Hay-on-Wye.

Other walks are detailed on: www.walking.visitwales.com

Outdoors

www.ccw.gov.uk The Countryside Council for Wales provides information on nature reserves and walking and riding paths.

www.cycling.visitwales.co.uk Excellent site for touring or mountain biking; even shows how steep the climbs are.

www.goodbeachguide.co.uk How to check your kid won't be bathing in sewage. Lists facilities and activities for a large number of recommended UK beaches.

www.sustrans.org.uk Official site of the charity that coordinates the National Cycle Network. With a clickable, zoom-in map.

www.walkingworld.com Perhaps the best directory of British walks, although you have to pay to download their detailed maps.

History, politics and culture

See also CADW, page 24.

www.castlewales.com Information and links to over 400 castles throughout Wales.

www.onehistoricgarden.co.uk Information on 7 historic gardens in Wales which are currently being regenerated: Bryngarw Country Park, Margam Country Park, Penllergare Valley Woods, Cwmdonkin Park, Aberglasney Gardens, Scolton Manor and Colby Woodland Garden.

Volunteer work

www.btcv.org.uk The British Trust for Conservation Volunteers provides volunteer opportunities, themed events and activities throughout the year.

www.cat.org.uk The Centre for Alternative Technology near Machynlleth relies on volunteers to keep the centre running.

www.rspb.org.uk The Royal Society for the Protection of Birds is a UK charity working to secure a healthy environment for birds and wildlife; volunteer opportunities.

www.wwoof.org Willing Workers on Organic Farms, volunteer opportunities for those interested in the organic movement.

Visas and immigration

Visa regulations are subject to change, so it is essential to check with your local British embassy, high commission or consulate before leaving home. Citizens of all European countries – except Albania, Bosnia Herzegovina, Kosovo, Macedonia, Moldova, Turkey, Serbia and all former Soviet republics (other than the Baltic states) – require only a passport to enter Britain and can generally stay for up to 3 months. Citizens of Australia, Canada, New Zealand, South Africa or the USA can stay for up to 6 months, providing they have a return ticket and sufficient funds to cover their stay. Citizens of most other countries require a visa from the commission or consular office in the country of application.

The **UK Border Agency**, www.ukba.homeoffice.gov.uk, is responsible for UK immigration matters and its website is a good place to start for anyone hoping visit, work, study or emigrate to the UK. For visa extensions also contact the UK Border Agency via the website. Citizens of Australia, Canada, New Zealand, South Africa or the USA wishing to stay longer than 6 months will need an Entry Clearance Certificate from the British High Commission in their country. For more details, contact your nearest British embassy, consulate or high commission, or the Foreign and Commonwealth Office in London.

Weights and measures

Imperial and metric systems are both in use. Distances on roads are measured in miles and yards, drinks poured in pints and gills, but generally, the metric system is used elsewhere.

Pembrokeshire & Gower

Contents

Footprint features

Swansea and the Gower

This is, above all, Dylan Thomas territory. The poet was born in the industrial city of Swansea and spent his final years further west in the evocative village of Laugharne, where his last home, the simple Boathouse, is set on a glorious silvery spot on the Taff Estuary. Most of his greatest works, including his 'play for voices', *Under Milk Wood*, were written and inspired by this little chunk of Wales and if you're a fan of his work – or want to learn more about it – then this is the place to come. In 2014 Swansea will be celebrating the 100th anniversary of his birth, with a programme of special events. For information see: www.dylanthomas.com and www.dt100.info.

Swansea itself has some worthwhile museums and the nearby resort of Mumbles offers a great choice of places to eat and drink. Best of all, for anyone looking for accessible yet unspoiled countryside, is the Gower Peninsula, a tourist hotspot famed for its award-winning surf beaches in the south, and its quieter marshlands in the north. This is a place best explored leisurely on foot or by bike.

Arriving in Swansea and the Gower

Getting there

Swansea is just off the M4, about 45 minutes' drive from Cardiff and 35 minutes' from Carmarthen. The central bus station, is right next to the city's Quadrant shopping centre. **National Express** ⓘ *T0871-781 8178, www.nationalexpress.com*, runs coaches to Swansea from most major towns and cities, as well as direct from Heathrow and Gatwick airports. **First Cymru** ⓘ *www.firstgroup.com*, operates the Swansea area bus routes. In addition, **Greyhound** ⓘ *www.greyhounduk.com*, operates an hourly service between Swansea and Cardiff bus stations and twice hourly from Bristol and Bristol Airport.

Swansea railway station is 10 minutes' walk north of the centre at the top of the high street. There are frequent direct train services to Swansea from Cardiff Central station; the journey takes approximately 40 minutes. There are also direct services from London (3½ hours), Manchester, Carmarthen and Fishguard Harbour. Swansea is also the southern terminus for the **Heart of Wales** line, www.heart-of-wales.co.uk, which runs across the top of the Gower to Llanelli, then up through Llandeilo and Llandovery to Shrewsbury. For travel information contact **Traveline Cymru** ⓘ *T0871-200 2233, www.traveline-cymru.info.*

Getting around

Swansea can easily be explored on foot. There are regular buses to Mumbles as well as the *Swansea Bay Rider*, a land train. The Gower is well served by buses from Swansea; North Gower is good for cycling as traffic is light.

Tourist information

Mumbles TIC ⓘ *Methodist Church, 520B Mumbles Rd, Mumbles, T01792-361302, www.mumblestic.co.uk, summer Mon-Sat 1000-1600, longer hours in school summer holidays, winter 1100-1600*, is a very helpful office with books on walking in the Gower. **Swansea TIC** ⓘ *Plymouth St, Swansea, by bus station, T01792-468321, www.visitswanseabay.com, Mon-Sat 0930-1730, Jul to mid-Sep also open Sun 1000-1600*, sells tickets for concerts, events, Greyhound travel and local bus tickets all year round. Useful websites include www.swanseacitycentre.com and www.swansea.gov.uk.

Swansea (Abertawe) and around → *For listings, see pages 36-39.*

Swansea, the second city of Wales, is a far more Welsh place than its great rival, Cardiff, and Welsh is spoken by far more people. Its origins go back to Norman times at least, when a castle was built here as part of William the Conqueror's strategy to suppress the troublesome Welsh. Its maritime location and proximity to Wales' rich coalfields led to its inevitable development as an industrial town. By the 18th century it was a thriving coal port, as well as a copper smelting centre. The city was very badly damaged by bombing in the Second World War and most of its historic heart was flattened. It might not be pretty enough to have you reaching for the camera but it's a relaxed city with a welcoming atmosphere. Dylan Thomas himself once described it as 'ugly', then later described it as 'marble town, city of laughter, little Dublin'.

Today, Swansea is re-inventing itself as a tourist spot, making use of natural features like its seemingly endless arc of sand. The city centre and Maritime Quarter (the former docks) have some fine collections in the art galleries and museums, and the traditional Labour Club on Wind Street now rubs shoulders with sharp bars and restaurants. High above the amphitheatre of Castle Square, sit the remains of Swansea Castle, which had its heydey in the 13th century but is still the focus for many outdoor events. If you've only one day to spend here, try not to make it Monday when most of the sights are closed.

Places in Swansea

The **Dylan Thomas Centre** ⓘ *Somerset Place, T01792-463980, www.dylandthomas.com, daily 1000-1630*, is based in a beautiful colonnaded Victorian listed building. It celebrates Thomas through memorabilia such as original manuscripts and letters and also hosts literature festivals, author readings, lectures and discussions. It has a good second-hand bookshop and a nice café.

Swansea's hot house, **Plantasia** ⓘ *Parc Tawe shopping complex, T01792-474555, daily 1000-1700, £3.95, children £2.95*, is home to 850 species of tropical and sub-tropical plants

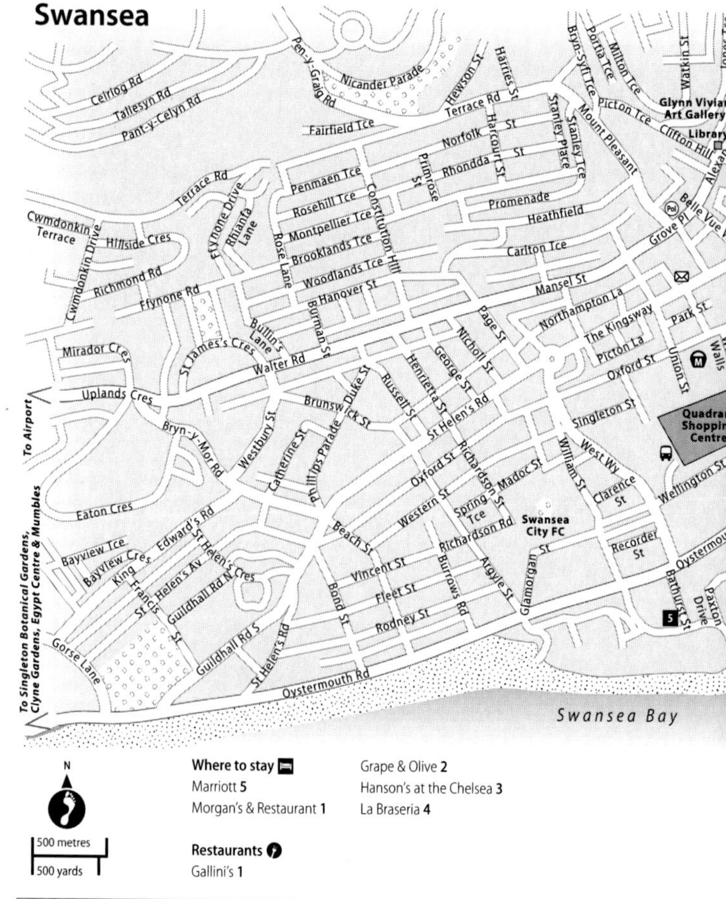

as well as tamarin monkeys, rainforest birds and butterflies, and other exotic animals. There are three different climate zones where you can find bananas, coconuts, giant bamboo, a wonderful lush collection of ferns and plenty of prickly cacti.

Located in the Old Maritime Quarter, the **Attic Gallery** ⓘ *37 Pocketts Wharf, Maritime Quarter, T01792-653387, www.atticgallery.co.uk, Tue-Fri 1000-1700, Sat 1000-1600*, is Wales' longest established private gallery; it highlights the work of some of the principality's most important artists and promotes new artists. The **Glynn Vivian Art Gallery** ⓘ *Alexandra Rd, T01792-516900, Tue-Sun 1000-1700, free*, has a good collection of work by 20th-century Welsh artists such as Ceri Richards and Gwen and Augustus John. There's also an internationally important collection of porcelain and china. Closed for major refurbishment until late 2014.

Swansea's newest museum is the **National Waterfront Museum** ⓘ *Swansea Marina, T02920-573600, www.museumwales.ac.uk, daily 1000-1700, free*. Built at a cost of £31 million, it covers the industrial history of Wales – and also takes a peep into the future. Galleries cover themes such as coal, metal and the sea and exhibits include a replica of the *Penydarren locomotive*, the world's first steam train. There's also an original copy of the 1851 census which stated that Wales was the world's first industrialized country. It covers two floors and has several cafés and lots of audiovisual exhibits, so it's great for kids.

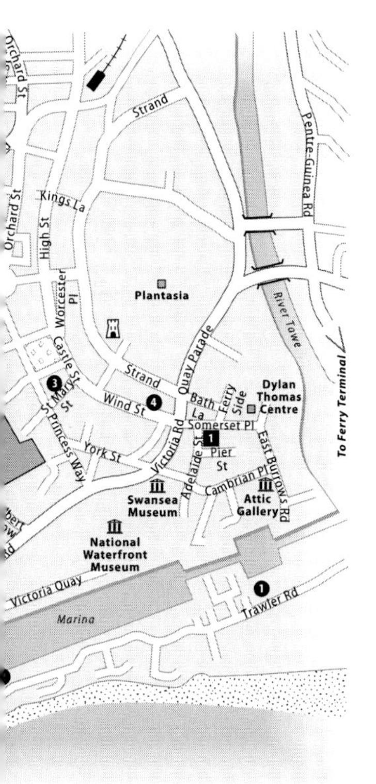

Swansea Museum ⓘ *Victoria Rd, T01792-653763, www.swansea.gov.uk, Tue-Sun 1000-1700, free*, is the oldest museum in Wales (Dylan Thomas called it 'a museum that should be in a museum'); it's best known for its ancient 2200-year-old mummy of a priest called Hor, but also has a good collection of Nantgarw pottery and porcelain. There's also a memorial to Edgar Evans, a Swansea man who was one of Captain Scott's companions on the ill-fated polar expedition. You will find more Egyptian antiquities at the **Egypt Centre** ⓘ *Taliesin Arts Centre, Swansea University, T01792-295960, www.egypt.swan.ac.uk, Tue-Sat 1000-1600, free*. There are more than 1000 artefacts dating as far back as 3500 BC, with statues of gods and goddesses, jewellery, the painted coffin of a musician from Thebes and even a mummified crocodile. Interesting even if you wouldn't know Tutunkhamen from Nefertiti.

Swansea Market ⓘ *off Castle Sq and the A4067, by the Quadrant Shopping Centre, Mon-Sat 0830-1700*, is the biggest covered market in Wales. Swansea's salty maritime heritage means you can come here to try local grub such as fresh cockles with loads of vinegar and pepper. It's renowned for fresh seafood from the estuary, as well as Welsh cheese, laver bread and bacon (Swansea's traditional breakfast dish) and freshly baked Welsh cakes. **Joe's Ice Cream**, also available in nearby Mumbles (where they even queue in the winter), is proclaimed by locals, and many sweet-toothed visitors, to be the best ice cream in the world.

Outside the town, **Singleton Botanical Gardens** ⓘ *located within the vast grounds of Singleton Park, T01792-298637, daily, winter 0900-1630, summer 0900-1800, Aug 0900-2000, free*, have glass houses for desert, temperate and tropical regions, as well as a herb garden, huge magnolias and ornamental gardens. In the economic greenhouse you can see lots of exotic plants that are of economic importance, such as sugar cane, olives, coffee and coconut.

On the Mumbles road, **Clyne Gardens** ⓘ *T01792-205327, daily, free*, is largely a woodland garden and covers 46 acres of land surrounding Clyne Castle, purchased in 1860 by millionaire William Graham Vivian. As well as a great collection of rhododendrons and azaleas there's a bog garden, wildflower meadow and bluebell wood. Considered to be at its best in May, it's a good place to bring kids and a picnic.

Mumbles (Mwmbwls)

ⓘ *www.visitswanseabay.com/mumbles.*

West of Swansea Bay and the gateway to the Gower, is the cheery stretch of seafront known as Mumbles (Dylan Thomas called it "a rather nice village, despite its name"). This name originally referred to a couple of little offshore islands and is a corruption of the name *mamelles* (breasts) that French sailors gave them. Today it's a general term for the village of **Oystermouth** (Ystumllwynarth), an historic oyster fishing port, and the long stretch of seafront to Mumbles Lighthouse and the blue-flag beach **Bracelet Bay**. It's noted for its generous number of pubs (some patronized by the ever-thirsty Mr Thomas) along the legendary Mumbles Mile and has some fine places to eat (see Restaurants, page 37). Nearby, **Caswell Bay** offers some great urban surfing. The winding streets behind the promenade contain the ruins of **Oystermouth Castle** ⓘ *Apr-Sep daily 1100-1700, £2.50, family £6*, a former Norman stronghold. The surrounding parkland offers great views out over the Mumbles headland and across the sweeping sands of Swansea Bay.

The Gower (Gwyr) → *For listings, see pages 36-39.*

West of Mumbles is the 19-mile-long Gower, a small and scenic peninsular, which resembles a toe dipping tentatively into the Bristol Channel. The Gower was Britain's first designated Area of Outstanding Natural Beauty and much of the coastline is owned by the National Trust. Its lovely beaches have become a favourite with surfers and windsurfers. Its cliff tops and narrow lanes offer some good walking – including the Gower Coastal Path (38 miles from Mumbles to Crofty; www.walescoastpath.gov.uk) – and cycling. The peninsula is sprinkled with ancient churches, small villages and lovely heathlands. If you want to escape the crowds make for the north coast, where there are lonely stretches of grazed saltmarshes, rich in rare plants.

The Gower is dotted with pretty and historic little churches; if you're interested in things ecclesiastical, pick up a copy of the leaflet '*In the Steps of the Saints*' which has details of all the Gower's churches. These include St Cadoc's, Cheriton – known as the Cathedral of the Gower, and St Mary's, Pennard, the burial place of Welsh poet Harri Webb. The website www.visitswanseabay.com/gower has some useful visitor information.

South Gower

Three Cliffs Bay is the closest of the Gower beaches to Swansea and has a glorious three-mile stretch of sand with dramatic rock formations, popular with climbers. At nearby Parkmill, on the main A4118 is the **Gower Heritage Centre** ⓘ *T01792-371206, www.gowerheritagecentre.co.uk, daily Apr-Oct 1000-1730, Nov-Mar 1000-1600, £5.95, children £4.95, family £21*, a child-orientated attraction based around an old water-powered corn mill, with craft workshops and displays, and a tea shop. The centre also offers guided walks for groups and has plenty of leaflets on the area; it's the place to take the kids on a rainy day.

Further round the peninsula is **Oxwich Bay**, a National Nature Reserve encompassing dunes, marshes and woodlands, as well as a popular sandy beach and plenty of accommodation. The relatively sheltered bay offers good opportunities for windsurfing; the surf picks up at high tide. Here you'll find **St Illtyd's Church** ⓘ *open 1100-1500*, which stands on the site of a sixth-century Celtic monastic cell, and **Oxwich Castle** ⓘ *(CADW) Apr-Sep, daily 1000-1700, £3*, the ruins of a Tudor manor.

A couple of miles on from Oxwich, the road brings you to the quiet village of **Horton**, which has a good beach, popular with windsurfers, and livelier but more touristy **Port Eynon**. At the western end of the beach, signposted from the YHA, is **Culver Hole**, a man-made cave built into the cliffs, thought to have been used by smugglers. From here the spectacular five-mile **Gower Coastal Path** winds its way around the cliff tops to Rhossili. Along the walk look out for **Paviland Cave**, where human remains were found dating back over 20,000 years.

The picturesque village of **Rhossili** is the end of the A4118 road, at the far western tip of the Gower Peninsula. Steps lead down to the vast three-mile stretch of sand that is **Rhossili Bay**, one of the most stunning beaches in the country (voted "10th best beach in the world" by TripAdvisor) and very popular with surfers. It's a good spot for lunch or a cream tea, and at low tide it's possible to walk out across the causeway to **Worm's Head**, a rocky outcrop supposedly resembling a Welsh dragon. Information and tide times are available from the **National Trust information centre** ⓘ *Coastguard Cottages, Rhossili, T01792-390707, daily Feb-Dec.*

North and west Gower

Along the northern stretch of Rhossili Bay a narrow road winds up to the little village of **Llangennith**. To get here by car follow the B4291 from Swansea, or if coming from South Gower, there's a cut through at **Reynoldston**. Llangennith can get very busy in summer with hoards of day trippers heading down to the beach. There's a good pub, surf shop and a little church, dedicated to St Cenydd who founded a priory here in the sixth century. Even older is the massive dolmen near Reynoldston known as **King Arthur's stone**, which sits alone on a windy ridge. A giant capstone, weighing around 25 tons, balanced on smaller rocks, it marks a Neolithic burial chamber. The views from this isolated spot seem to stretch forever.

Swansea and the Gower listings

For hotel and restaurant price codes and other relevant information, see pages 15-19.

Where to stay

Swansea *p31, map p32*

££££-£££ Morgan's Hotel, Somerset Place, T01792-484848, www.morganshotel.co.uk. This was always Catherine Zeta-Jones and Michael Douglas's hotel of choice and the place to come if you want to treat yourself. Rooms are named after local ships and are individually designed. There are lovely wooden floors, comfy beds with crisp sheets, and plasma TVs set into the walls. Bathrooms have scented candles and lovely big baths. There's also a swish restaurant.

££££-££ Marriott Hotel, Maritime Quarter, T01792-642020, www.marriott.co.uk. Its location redeems the uninspiring exterior of this 4-star chain hotel with 122 rooms, small swimming pool, sauna and fitness equipment. It is well placed next to the marina and most rooms have lovely views, either of the marina or Swansea Bay. Ask for a view when you book.

££ Chatcoombe, 20 Rhyd-y-Defaid Drive, Sketty, T01792-207100, www.visitswansea bay.com/chatcoombe. This a small, friendly 4-star B&B on the outskirts of the city

Mumbles *p34*

£££ Patrick's with Rooms, 638 Mumbles Rd, T01792-360199, www.patrickswithrooms. com. 16 en suite rooms, each individually furnished and all facing the sea. Convenient for the sleek restaurant downstairs.

££ Glenview Guest House, 140 Langland Rd, T01792-367933, www.mumblesglen view. co.uk. B&B in a Victorian house overlooking Underhill Park. It has en suite rooms, pretty gardens and real fires in the lounge in winter.

££ Tides Reach, 388 Mumbles Rd, T01792-404877, www.tidesreachguesthouse.com. High-quality 5-star B&B on the seafront. All rooms en suite and extremely clean and comfortable. The lounge has good views over the bay and is furnished with antiques.

Gower *p34*

££££ Fairyhill, Reynoldstone, T01792-390139 or T0871-995 8220, www.fairyhill. net. This is the Gower's only 5-star hotel but its reputation has spread much further. An ivy covered, 18th-century house tucked away in the quiet of the countryside; it's a great place to treat yourself and luxuriate – if you can afford it.

££ King Arthur Hotel, Higher Green, Reynoldston, T01792-390775, www.king arthurhotel.co.uk. Lovely refurbished rooms at this warm and popular inn, situated on the village green. Ask for a room in the annexe and you won't have to worry about noise from the bar.

Camping

Campsites in the Gower are very popular and often full at weekends during the summer, phone ahead for availability or arrive early on Fri. See www.the-gower.com/campsites or www.gower-camping.co.uk for further information. Some good sites include:

Bank Farm Leisure Park, Horton, T01792-390228, www.visitswanseabay.com/ bankfarmleisurepark. Family-run park overlooking Port Eynon Bay with stunning sea views. Outdoor heated swimming pool with retractable roof.

Greenways, Oxwich, T01792-390220, www. visitswanseabay.com/greenways. 4-star camping park with views over Oxwich Bay.

Restaurants

Swansea *p31, map p32*

£££ Morgans, Somerset Place, T01792-484848, www.morganshotel.co.uk. This is Swansea's special-occasion venue. There are 2 restaurants in this upmarket hotel that's situated in the former Victorian Port Authority building.

££ Hanson at the Chelsea, 17 St Mary St, T01792-464068, www.hansonatthechelsea.co.uk. Lots of fresh Welsh produce at this popular restaurant which serves lots of seafood. There's a separate veggie menu and lots of diet-defying desserts such as bread and butter pudding.

££-£ Grape and Olive, Meridian Tower, Trawler Rd, T01792-462617, www.swansea.grapeandolive.co.uk. Come for relaxed brunches, lunches and evening meals to the top floor of the tallest building in Wales with views over the waterfront.

££-£ La Braseria, 28 Wind St, T01792-469683, www.labraseria.com. Situated on Wind St, the heart of Swansea's drinking and dining area, this large restaurant/wine bar serves Mediterranean-influenced fresh meat and fish dishes. It's popular so gets busy.

£ Gallini's, Unit 3, Fishmarket Quay, Pilot's House Wharf, Swansea Marina, T01792-465285, www.gallinisrestaurant.co.uk. Perched on the quayside, this popular Italian café has a family-run restaurant on the 1st floor serving traditional Italian food in the evenings.

Mumbles *p34*

£££-££ PA's Wine Bar, 95 Newton Rd, T01792-367723, www.paswinebar.co.uk. This little wine bar serves Welsh food in a relaxed setting and is very popular. In summer the doors open and you can look out on to the garden. They do lots of fish, bought from the market – you might find Penclawdd mussels with white wine and garlic on the menu.

£££-££ Patrick's with Rooms, 638 Mumbles Rd, T01792-360199. Daily 1200-1400, Mon-Sat 1830-2150. Imaginative British cuisine in this very popular restaurant with accommodation . There's a daily specials board and they use lots of Welsh produce like cockles, laverbread and Welsh beef. Dishes might include pan-fried duck with honey plum sauce, or game pie, and they also have a good choice for veggies with things like ravioli with wild mushrooms.

£ Café Valance, 50 Newton Rd, T01792-367711. Great café with lots of comfy sofas and a good choice of filled baguettes, paninis, cakes and coffees.

£ The Coffee Denn, 34 Newton Rd, T01792-360044. Good place for snacks, light meals like jacket potatoes, and heartier options such as chicken casserole or cottage pie.

£ Verdi's Knab Rock, Mumbles Rd, T01792-369135, www.verdis-café.co.uk. Relaxed Italian ice cream parlour and restaurant, with great views across Swansea Bay. Great for relaxing outside with an ice cream sundae, pizzas, foccacia or just coffee.

Delis and takeaways

Deli 28, Newton Rd, T01792-366828. This is a great place to pick up cheeses, olives and other picnic items.

Gower *p34*

£££ Fairyhill, Reynoldstone off B4295, T01792-390139, www.fairyhill.net. If you can't afford to spend the night at this luxurious country hotel you can still enjoy some of its comforts in the restaurant, which uses local produce and serves classical food with a contemporary twist. Good choice of wines and delicious desserts too.

£££ Welcome to Town Inn, Llanrhidian, Gower, T01792-390015, www.thewelcometotown.co.uk. Highly acclaimed food at this award-winning bistro. Lots of Welsh produce on the menu. There's a good choice of Welsh cheeses, home-made bread and fresh vegetables. Also offer cookery masterclasses.

££-£ King Arthur Hotel, Higher Green, Reynoldston, T01792-390775. Lively inn on the village green, with a nautical theme in the cosy bar. Wide choice of bar meals with several veggie options.

£ Three Cliffs Coffee Shop, 68 Southgate Rd, Penard, off A4118 near Southgate, T01792-233885. Marble-top tables, outside seating and good home baking at this lovely little café tucked away on the south Gower coast. Serves a good selection of filled baguettes, snacks and coffees.

A rugby nation

Until their victory in the 2005 Six Nations Championship the Welsh rugby team had taken a bit of a battering. The glory days of the 1970s, when the Welsh game basked in the triumphs of players like Gareth Edwards and JPR Williams, had seemed well over.

The bell had appeared to toll for Welsh rugby with the arrival of professionalism in 1995. Once the game became a business, something of its gutsy spirit was lost, and Wales found it hard to find a foothold in this acquisitive commercial world. However, in recent years, Welsh rugby has regained its sparkle and there's a new confidence and pride in the game. The Millennium Stadium, a state-of-the-art venue, constructed bang in the centre of Cardiff, was built to replace the legendary Cardiff Arms Park, scene of many Welsh rugby wins (for 28 years the English side did not win once in Cardiff). In 2013 it was the venue for a decisive Welsh win over England, making Wales Six Nations' Champions – with full-back Leigh Halfpenny voted Player of the Championship.

Although hugely popular throughout the country, the notion of Wales as a rugby nation was never entirely accurate. In terms of clubs and top players, the game was mainly the preserve of the industrialized south. In the rural north, football (soccer), an import from nearby Liverpool and Manchester, took precedence.

So football versus rugby? Chances are the two passions will run side by side, just as they always have. Welsh Women's Rugby is also doing well. And if you want proof that the game still rouses intense passions, look no further than the Welsh rugby fan who, many years ago, was so convinced England would beat his team that he told his mates he would 'cut his balls off' if they won. Wales won – and he did. For further information look up **Welsh Rugby Union**, www.wru.co.uk.

What to do

Boat trips

Gower Coast Adventures, T07866-250440, www.gowercoastadventures.co.uk. Jet boat trips from Port Eynon Bay to Worms Head and Knab Rock, Mumbles to Three Cliffs Bay. Reductions for children and families.

River Tawe Boat Cruises, T07785-347549, www.scbt.org.uk. Discover Swansea's heritage in a 2-hr cruise from Swansea Marina and along the River Tawe.

Cycling

The **Millennium Coastal Park**, www.millenniumcoastalpark.com, has a 20-km cycle trail along the Loughor Estuary and runs from Bynea in the east to Pembury in the west.

Action Bikes, St David's Sq, T01792-464640. Located in the city centre a short distance from the start of the Swansea Bike Path, which runs 6 miles from the marina to Mumbles.

The Bike Hub, St Helen's Rd, T01792-466944. Offers bike hire and repairs.

Pedalabikeaway, North Dock, Llanelli, T01554-780123, www.pedalabikeaway.com. Has everything from mountain bikes to tandems for hire.

General activities

Clyne Farm, Westport Av, Mayals, Swansea, T01792-403333, www.clynefarm.com. Weekend and school holiday activity days. Can include archery, riding, indoor climbing – booking necessary. Also offers hacks and beach rides.

Horse riding

Parc le Breos, Parkmill, Gower, T01792-371636, www.parc-le-breos.co.uk. Daily rides and pony trekking holidays, as well as good-quality accommodation.

Watersports

360 Beach and Watersports, Mumbles Rd, Swansea, T01792-655844, www.360swansea.co.uk. Open all year and situated on Swansea Bay close to the city centre. Ideal for novices looking to try an activity for the first time.

Oxwich Watersports, The Beach Hut, Oxwich, T07740-284079, www.visitswanseabay.com/oxwichwatersports. Mar-Oct 1000-1700. Offers a variety of watersports in Oxwich Bay.

PJs Surf Shop, Llangennith, Gower, T01792-386669. Good range of wetsuits and surfboards for hire.

Welsh Surf School, Llangennith, Gower, T01792-386426, www.wsfsurfschool.co.uk. Run surfing lessons in Rhossili Bay.

Carmarthenshire

Carmarthenshire is often overlooked by visitors rushing westwards to Pembrokeshire or north to Snowdonia. However, it's one of the most Welsh parts of Wales – green, rural, with fine gardens, the poignant ruins of ancient castles and a landscape steeped in myth and legend. The Welsh language is still widely spoken here. It's perhaps appropriate that the national poet, Dylan Thomas, chose to live in Carmarthenshire and a visit to his former home in Laugharne on the soft, sleepy coastline is a highlight of any trip to Wales.

Arriving in Carmarthenshire

Getting there and around

Carmarthen has good public transport links (T01267-234567 for information). **National Expressi** ⓘ *www.nationalexpress.com, runs 2 daily buses from Swansea and Haverfordwest, and a daily bus from Aberystwyth.* The **Beacons Bus** ⓘ *www.travelbreconbeacons.info/beacons-bus*, links Carmarthen with Brecon in the summer months. Trains run from Cardiff, Fishguard, Pembroke, Haverfordwest and Milford Haven. The **Heart of Wales** train line ⓘ *www.heart-of-wales.co.uk*, travels from Swansea, through Llanelli and follows the Tywi Valley up through Llandeilo and Llandovery, to Shrewsbury. Trains to Pembrokeshire also pass through Carmarthen.

Tourist information

Carmarthen TIC ⓘ *Old Castle House, Carmarthen, T01267-231557, www.visit.carmarthenshire.gov.uk, check for hours.* **Llandovery Heritage Centre** ⓘ *Kings Rd, Llandovery, T01550-720693.*

Carmarthen (Caerfyrddin) and around → *For listings, see page 44.*

Often regarded as the gateway to west Wales, the town on the River Tywi (also known by its anglicized name, Towy) is the ancient capital of the region. Although it was founded as a Roman fort, legend claims that it is the birthplace of Merlin (Myrddin). Once a busy trading port and wool town, Carmarthen is now a flourishing market town and stronghold of the Welsh language. Sights of interest within the town include the **Oriel Myrddin** ⓘ *Church Lane, T01267-222775, www.orielmyrddingallery.co.uk, Mon-Sat 1000-1700, free*, a craft centre and imaginative gallery showcasing local artists.

Around Carmarthen

Two miles east of Carmarthen, the former seat of the Bishop of St David's between 1542 and 1974, now houses the regional history museum. The **Carmarthenshire County Museum** ⓘ *Bishop's Palace, Abergwili, T01267-228696, check opening times before visiting, free*, has an interesting and eclectic exhibition of well-presented displays of local castles, pottery and archaeological finds, wooden dresses, and the origins of one of Wales's first eisteddfodau (Welsh cultural festivals), held nearby in 1450.

Three miles north of Carmarthen, on the A484, is the **Gwili Railway** ⓘ *T01267-238213, www.gwili-railway.co.uk, Apr-Oct, times and days vary, £9, £3 children, £20 family*. This steam railway starts at Bronwydd Arms and follows a river much of the way, before stopping at Llwyfan Cerrig, where there's a picnic site and miniature railway. You can get off here or continue to Danycoed and return. The round trip is four miles.

National Botanic Garden of Wales

ⓘ *Llanarthne, T01558-668768, www.gardenofwales.org.uk, summer daily 1000-1800, winter 1000-1630, £8.50, children £4.50, family £21.*

Opened in May 2000, this is one of Wales' most important millennium projects – its own botanic garden. It's a bit like a mix of Kew and the Eden Project – though on a smaller scale. The Middleton estate on which it's built dates from the 1600s and the old double-walled garden (cleverly designed so as to produce more heat) has been restored and has beds containing all sorts of vegetables and flowers, with interesting old varieties like yellow raspberries and funny shaped tomatoes. Special events and exhibitions are held throughout the year. You might, for example, learn about the Physicians of Myddfai – the name referring to a line of Welsh physicians who used natural remedies to cure people. There are displays on herbal remedies/treatments from all over the world. There's also a 19th-century apothecaries' hall from Anglesey – complete with bottles with labels like 'Dr Rooke's Solar Elixir and Reanimating Balm of Life'. At the heart of the garden is the Great Glasshouse designed by Norman Foster. This is divided into different climate zones, with plants from Australia, South Africa, the Mediterranean, Canary Islands, Chile and California. Other attractions include a summer 'maize maze', a Japanese garden and a bog garden.

Llandeilo and around

→ *For listings, see page 44.*

Llandeilo is a small market town in the Tywi Valley. It's just a mile from Dinefwr Castle and about four miles from Carreg Cennan Castle so makes a convenient spot for a bite to eat if you're exploring the area.

Aberglasney Gardens

ⓘ *Llangathen, 2 miles west of Llandeilo, T01558-668998, www.aberglasney.org, daily summer 1000-1800, winter 1030-1600, £8, children £4, family £20.*

East of Middleton, off the A40, is Wales' answer to Heligan – a lost garden surrounding a fine manor house, both of which had suffered badly from neglect and looked doomed to disappear. Both the house – a listed building – and the weed-choked grounds, were saved in the mid-1990s and a unique garden was discovered, which has now been carefully restored. The formal Cloister Gardens are a rare and authentic Jacobean survival, as almost all such gardens were swept away in the 18th century. You can also see Victorian aviaries, a Pool Garden, Kitchen Garden and an atmospheric Yew Tunnel. There's a good café where you can sit outside on fine days.

Dinefwr Castle and Park and Newton House

ⓘ *West of Llandeilo, T01558-824512, May to end Aug castle 1000-1600, house and grounds 1100-1800, otherwise house closes at 1600, check hours before visiting; house and grounds National Trust £3.20, children £1.80, family £8.60; castle CADW free.*

Legend has it that the first castle at Dinefwr was built in AD 877 by Rhodri Mawr, King of Wales. It became the principal court of Hywel Dda (the 'Good') who in AD 920 ruled much of

Southwest Wales, known as Deheubarth. He was responsible for creating the first uniform legal system in Wales. The ruined stone castle visible today was built on the same site and was the 12th-century stronghold of Lord Rhys, who united Welsh rulers against the English.

In the 17th century the more comfortable Newton House was built (about a 25-minute walk across parkland from the castle), and the park was landscaped in the 1770s by Capability Brown. The house has been restored by the National Trust and you can see the period rooms, hung with paintings. The park is notable for its indigenous rare White Park cattle, which are white with long horns and black noses. They have a lineage stretching back to the time of Hywel Dda – in the event of any injury to the King of Deheubarth tribute had to be paid in the form of these cattle.

Aberdeunant

This tiny **traditional farmhouse** ⓘ *(NT) Taliaris, 3 miles north of Llandeilo, T01558-650177, Apr-Sep, 1st Sat and Sun of each month, tours 1200-1700, £2, children £1, tours must be booked in advance*, gives a rare insight into a rural way of life that's now been lost. Guided tours are available, but it's so small only a few people can fit into it at once.

Carreg Cennen Castle

ⓘ *(CADW) Southeast of Llandeilo, near Trapp, T01558-822291, Easter-Oct daily 0930-1830, Nov to end Mar daily 0930-dusk, £4, children £3.50, family £12.*

Carreg Cennen is probably the most dramatically situated castle in Wales – perched high on a precipitous crag above the River Cennen, the views down the valley are stunning. Legend has it that a castle was built here by King Arthur's knights; one of them is still said to sleep under the existing structure, a seemingly impenetrable stone stronghold which dates from around 1300. It was dismantled by the Yorkists in the Wars of the Roses and is now a romantic ruin. A visit here includes taking a torch and walking along the dark passageway that leads to a cave beneath the fort.

Llandovery and around

→ *For listings, see page 44.*

In the northern part of Carmarthenshire, Llandovery is a good base for exploring the **Twyi Valley**. The town was once an important stopping place for drovers taking cattle to market in London; it was so important that a drover's bank, the Bank of the Black Ox, was founded here. In 1909 it became part of Lloyds Bank. The town has Roman origins, though the site of the Roman fort is now occupied by **St Mary's Church** at Llanfair-ar-y-Bryn just north of the town. William Williams Pantycelyn, one of Wales most famous composers of hymns (he wrote '*Guide me O Thou Great Jehovah*') is buried there.

Dolaucothi Gold Mines

ⓘ *(NT) Pumsaint, Llanwrda, T01558-650177, Easter to end Oct daily 1000-1700, £5.45, children £2.60, family £13.16.*

To the northeast of Llandovery, the Dolaucothi Gold Mines were first mined by the Romans. These ancient gold mines were opened again in the 19th century and worked until 1938. There are underground tours, exhibitions and a chance to pan for gold.

Talley Abbey

A 10-minute drive southwest of the mines, off the B4302, is remote Talley Abbey, founded in 1185. The building project ran out of money early on and the abbey was never as large as was first envisaged. It was an early victim of Edward I's assault on Wales and was later dissolved by Henry VIII. It had become a ruin by the 19th century and is a lonely sight today – little more than a shell.

Carmarthenshire Coast → *For listings, see page 44.*

The coastline of Carmarthenshire has a different character to the wild interior and is notable as the final home of Dylan Thomas, who spent his last years in the simple boathouse at Laugharne. As you travel west from the Gower along the A484 over the Loughor Estuary, you come to the excellent **National Wetland Centre** ⓘ *Penclacwydd, Llwynhendy, near Llanelli, T01554-741087, www.wwt.org.uk, summer daily 0930-1700, £7.91, children £4.36, family £22.09.* This is twitcher heaven, but you don't have to be a bino-clutching beardie to enjoy a visit. The centre covers 450 acres around the Burry Inlet, with salt marshes, mudflats and a landscaped area that's home to flamingos, geese and ducks. Hides give you the opportunity to see a wide range of wildfowl and wading birds; in winter around 50,000 birds come here. Species you might spot include herons, ringed plovers and little egrets. There's also a good interactive **Discovery Centre** for kids and a café.

Further west, just off the A484, is one of Wales' lesser-known castles, well-preserved **Kidwelly** ⓘ *(CADW), Castle St, T01554-890104, Oct-Easter 0930-1600, Easter-Sep Mon-Sat 0930-1800, Sun 1100-1600, £3.50, family £10.10.* Founded by the Normans, the castle was a link in a chain of coastal strongholds. Its most prominent feature is the great gatehouse, completed in 1422.

Laugharne (Talacharn)

The undoubted highlight of the Carmarthenshire coast, described by Dylan Thomas as "a legendary lazy little black magical bedlam by the sea" – and the most likely inspiration for fictional Llareggub of *Under Milk Wood*, which he wrote here. (He was having a sly joke when he came up with the name – spell it backwards and you'll see why.) On this glorious spot on the Taff Estuary, you can feel the spirit of this most quotable of poets. He came here several times, once to chase after Caitlin – whom he later married – and lived in several houses around the town until in 1949 his benefactor, Margaret Taylor, bought him and his family the famous Boathouse where he lived until his death in 1953. **The Dylan Thomas Boathouse** ⓘ *Dylan's Walk, T01994-427420, www.dylanthomasboathouse.com, daily May-Oct 1000-1730, Nov-Apr 1030-1530, £4, children £1.95, family £9,* is a simple building with an idyllic location, perched on the clifftop with glorious views over the estuary and its "heron-priested shores". It's reached by a narrow track from the town but is so poorly signposted you're sure to miss it at first. His tiny writing shed, originally a garage, is laid out much as it was when Thomas worked here, with scrunched up pieces of paper and a bottle of beer on the table. The house itself is the simply furnished living room, with some copies of his manuscripts and other memorabilia. Nearby, in the township is **St Martin's Churchyard**, where Thomas and his wife are buried.

Close to the Boathouse, on the shore, is **Laugharne Castle** ⓘ *(CADW), T01994-427906, Apr-Sep daily 1000-1700, £3.80, concessions £2.85, family £11.40,* an atmospheric ruin built in the mid- to late-13th century. In Elizabethan times it was turned into a mansion, but after the Civil War it fell into decline. JMW Turner painted it and Dylan Thomas sometimes worked in its summerhouse.

A short drive inland from Laugharne is the village of **St Clears**, which is worth stopping off to explore for an hour or so.

Carmarthenshire listings

For hotel and restaurant price codes and other relevant information, see pages 15-19.

Where to stay

Carmarthen and around *p40*

£££ Glasfryn, Brechfa, T01267-202306, www.glasfrynguesthousebrechfa.co.uk. 3 en suite rooms at this little village B&B. Evening meals available.

£££ Ivy Bush Royal Hotel, Spilman St, T01267-235111, www.ivybushroyal.co.uk. Refurbished hotel, once a retreat for Nelson and Lady Hamilton. Rooms are well equipped and comfortable with standard hotel furnishings.

£££ Ty Mawr Country House, Brechfa, near Carmarthen, T01267-202332, www.wales-country-hotel.co.uk. There's a lovely rural feel to this ancient whitewashed farmhouse with original beams and log fires. It's noted for its good Welsh food, which is mostly organic.

£££-££ Coedllys, Llangynin, St Clears, T01994-231455, www.coedllyscountryhouse.co.uk. Just 3 guest rooms at this guesthouse in a rural valley – a great base for birdwatchers.

££ Allt y Golau Uchaf, Felingwm Uchaf, T01267-290455, www.alltygolau.com. Comfortable and clean rooms in this restored farmhouse in a peaceful location. Immaculate residents' lounge.

££ Lolfa Cynin, Llangynin Rd, St Clears, T01994-231516, www.lolfacynin.co.uk. This working farm offers unexpectedly plush accommodation – it even has a spa and a swimming pool.

Laugharne and around *p43*

££££ Browns Hotel, King St, T01994-427688, www.browns-hotel.co.uk. This hotel was once a favourite haunt of Dylan Thomas. At the time of writing it is being refurbished, but is due to re-open mid-2013. The New Three Mariners Inn is here too.

££££ The Corran Resort and Spa, East Marsh, off A4066 near Laugharne, T01994-427417, www.thecorran.com. Formerly Hurst House, this hotel re-opened in 2013. It offers contemporary luxury, with accommodation in the main house as well as suites in a converted barn. Aimed at the wealthy weekender market, it has a spa and restaurant too.

£££ Coedllys Country House, Llangynin, near St Clears, T01994-231455, www.coedllyscountryhouse.co.uk. This cosy retreat in the heart of the countryside is a great place to get away from it all. 3 en suite rooms.

£££ Llwyn Hall, Llwynhendy, Llanelli, T01554-777754, www.llynhall.com. Lovely old house with lots of antiques and fine furnishings. It's next door to the wildlife reserve.

Restaurants

Carmarthen and around *p40*

£££-££ Halfway Inn, Nantgaredig, T01558-668337, www.halfwayinn-carmarthen.co.uk. Standard bar lunches, and more filling meals like pan fried duck or braised lamb shank. Some veggie choices.

£££-££ Ty Mawr, Brechfa, T01267-202332, www.wales-country-hotel.co.uk. Restaurant with rooms with lots of Welsh lamb and beef on the menu, and several vegetarian options. Desserts include fresh farmhouse cheeses.

£££-££ Y Polyn, Nantgaredig, T01276-290000, www.ypolynrestaurant.co.uk. Lots of fresh Welsh produce on the menu in this pub which has both a restaurant and bar. Serves real ales too. No credit cards.

Laugharne and around *p43*

££ The Cors, Newbridge Rd, T01994-427219, www.thecors.co.uk. Booking essential. Highly rated food at this cosy restaurant with rooms offering contemporary Welsh dishes such as salt marsh lamb, or organic beef; let them know in advance if you're veggie.

Pembrokeshire

Everyone loves Pembrokeshire: sun-tanned surfers, bearded birdwatchers, history lovers and families all flock here. No wonder it's been dubbed the 'new Cornwall'. Its craggy cliffs, honeyed beaches and offshore islands make its coastline one of the finest in Britain. There are plenty of cultural attractions when you want a break from the beach, from the cathedral at St David's to ancient archaeological sites, castles and sleepy churches. And inland there are tranquil nooks like the Gwaun Valley, a pastoral haven that many overlook.

Arriving in Pembrokeshire

Getting there

There are good road links from the M4 and the south via the A40 from Haverfordwest to Fishguard. The A487 leads northeast up the coast towards Cardigan Bay and Aberystwyth. **National Express** ⓘ *www.nationalexpress.com*, runs buses from Swansea to Tenby, Pembroke, Haverfordwest and Steynton (for Milford Haven). St David's can only be reached by bus with **Richards Brothers** ⓘ *www.richardbrothers.co.uk*, from Haverfordwest or fishguard; it is also the last stop of the **Puffin Shuttle** (see below), which runs during the summer.

There are train stations at Tenby, Haverfordwest, Milford Haven, Fishguard and Pembroke, with direct daily services from Swansea and Carmarthen.

Ferries from Rosslare in Ireland run to Pembroke Dock (10 minutes from Pembroke) and Fishguard. ▸▸ *See Transport, page 61.*

Getting around

The area is served by **First Cymru** ⓘ *www.firstcymru.co.uk*, **Richards Brothers** ⓘ *T01239-613756, www.richardbros.co.uk*, and **Silcox Coaches** ⓘ *T01646-683143*. During the summer public transport along the coastal path is pretty good with bus services linking the main areas. The **Coastal Cruiser** bus service runs all year round (daily May to September, two buses a week October to April) between Pembroke, Angle, Freshwater West, Bosherston, Stackpole and Freshwater East. There are other buses running daily in summer: the **Poppit Rocket** runs from Cardigan to Fishguard; the **Strumble Shuttle** runs from Marloes to St David's; the **Puffin Shuttle** runs along the coast from Milford Haven to St David's; and the **Celtic Coaster** runs around St David's Peninsula. Details are available from TICs or from the websites www.pembrokeshire.gov.uk and www.pembrokeshiregreenways.co.uk. As you head inland it's generally easier to get around if you've got your own transport.

The cheapest way to travel is to buy a **West Wales Rover** ticket, £7, children £3.50, for all day travel on any of these buses and can be purchased on the bus. Weekly rover tickets cost £28 (children £14). For further information, see www.pembrokeshiregreenways.co.uk, www.sirgaerfyrddin.gov.uk or call **TravelineCymru** ⓘ *T0871-200 2233, www.traveline-cymru.info.*

Pembrokeshire Coast Path

The Pembrokeshire Coast Path is a long-distance waymarked walking trail, which clings to the stunning coastline of the Pembrokeshire National Park. It stretches 186 miles (299 km) between Amroth in the south to St Dogmaels in the north. It takes in a National Nature Reserve, a Marine Nature Reserve and 17 Sites of Special Scientific Interest (SSSIs). Walking it gives you the best chance of seeing the wildflowers, sea birds and seals that inhabit coastal Pembrokeshire. There are some steep ascents and descents so some sections are quite challenging. The whole route can be walked in a couple of weeks, and individual sections can be done as day walks. If you want to walk the path do make sure you plan it carefully, checking tide times locally, working out how far you can comfortably walk in one day, booking accommodation in advance, and making sure you have good maps, boots etc. Going from north to south the route can be split into easy chunks.

Day 1 St Dogmaels to Newport (approx 16 miles) – the most challenging section of the walk (less fit walkers should do this over two days, staying overnight at Moylegrove).

Day 2 Newport to Goodwick (approx 13 miles) – clifftops and some minor roads (this can be done over two days, staying overnight at Dinas, near Pwllgwaelod).

Day 3 Goodwick to Trefin (approx 19 miles) – a long section over high clifftops (can be done over two days with an overnight stay at Pwll Deri).

Day 4 Trefin to Whitesands (approx 11 miles) – a very popular stretch, takes you past pretty Porthgain, with the remains of old industry and a great pub. If you want to stay overnight at St David's it's easiest to stop at Caerfai.

Day 5 Whitesands to Solva (approx 13 miles) – one of the most popular stretches, with no road walking, above Whitesands Bay and round to St Bride's Bay.

Tourist information

Opening hours were under review at the time of writing; check out www.pembrokeshireinformationcentres.co.uk for details. **Tenby TIC** ⓘ *Upper Park Rd, Tenby, T01834-842404, tenby.tic@pembrokeshire.gov.uk, Apr-May 1000-1700, Jun-Sep 1000-1730, Jul-Aug 1000-2100, Oct 1000-1700, Nov-Apr 1000-1600*. **Pembroke** ⓘ *The Commons Rd, Pembroke, T01437-776499, pembroke.tic@pembrokeshire.gov.uk, Jun-Sep 1000-1730, otherwise 1000-1700*. **Newport TIC** ⓘ *Long St, T01239-820912, Newporttic@pembrokeshirecoast.org.uk, Apr-Sep Mon-Sat 1000-1730, shuts for lunch*. **St David's TIC/National Park Visitor Centre** ⓘ *Oriel y Parc, St David's, T01437-720392, www.stdavids.co.uk, Apr-Oct daily 0930-1700, Nov-Mar Mon-Sat 1000-1700, daily Apr-Oct 0930-1730, Mon-Sat Nov-Mar 1000-1600*. **Fishguard TIC** ⓘ *The Library, High St, T01348-873484, www.fishguard.tic@pembrokeshire.gov.uk, Easter-May daily 1000-1700, Jun-Sep daily 0930-1700, Oct Mon-Sat 1000-1700, Nov-Easter Mon-Sat 1000-1600*. **Haverfordwest Visitor Centre** ⓘ *Old Bridge St, T01437-763110, haverfordwest.tic@pembrokeshire.gov.uk, Easter-Oct Mon-Sat 0930-1730; Jul-Aug also Sun 1000-1600; Mon-Sat 1000-1600 at all other times*. Useful websites include: www.pembrokeshirecoast.org.uk, www.visitpembrokeshire.com and www.activitypembrokeshire.com.

Day 6 Solva to Little Haven (approx 12 miles) – some road walking on this section, which takes you past Newgale Sands.

Day 7 Little Haven to Dale (approx 20 miles) – this long stretch could be split over two days, with a stop at Marloes.

Day 8 Dale to Neyland, by Milford Haven (approx 15.5 miles) – lower cliffs and quite a bit of road walking, involves a causeway crossing that can only be crossed at low tide.

Day 9 Neyland to Angle (approx 15.5 miles) – more road walking involved, can split into two days, with an overnight stop at Pembroke.

Day 10 Angle to Bosherston (approx 18 miles) – no road walking on this section which takes you past popular spots like Barafundle Bay and Stackpole Quay.

Day 11 Bosherston to Manorbier (approx 11 miles) – a very popular section and a good day walk, can be combined with a visit to Manorbier Castle.

Day 12 Manorbier to Amroth (approx 15 miles) – the last stretch if you've done it north to south, but worth doing over two days and stopping at the charming resort of Tenby, which is about halfway along.

Practicalities

Baggage transport is well worth considering, unless you enjoy lugging a pack around. Call Tony's Taxis, T01437-720931, www.tonystaxis.co.uk.

Drover Holidays, T01497 821134, www.droverholidays.co.uk, offers self-guided walking holidays with baggage transfers.

You can also use public transport to help do the walk or sections of it: www.pembrokeshiregreenways.co.uk. Maps that cover this area are *OS Explorer OL 35/36*.

For further information covering everything from maps to where to stay, contact the National Park Authority, T0845-345 7275, www.nt.pcnpa.org.uk, or www.pembrokeshirecoast.org.uk.

Background

Pembrokeshire has been inhabited since at least Neolithic times and the north of the county in particular is still dotted with mysterious reminders of its prehistoric past. The **Preseli Hills** (Mynydd Preseli) – a brooding range of hills south of Newport – was an important Celtic stronghold and it was from here that the bluestones of Stonehenge were quarried. **Pentre Ifan**, a vast Neolithic burial chamber, is the most impressive of a number of cromlechs (tombs) that have survived. In the fifth and sixth centuries, early Christian missionaries began to arrive in western Wales. The most notable was St David, the patron saint of Wales, who founded St David's Cathedral in AD 550. It became an important place of pilgrimage and two visits here were considered to be equal to one pilgrimage to Rome.

Norse invaders periodically attacked Pembrokeshire, colonizing the most fertile lands in the south and giving distinctive Viking names to outlying islands such as **Skomer** and **Grassholm**, now renowned for their rich birdlife. The Vikings were followed by the Normans, who arrived late in the 11th century and consolidated their hold on the south by building a line of fortifications through the heart of the county. Known as the **Landsker** (frontier) it effectively divided Pembroke into a Celtic, Welsh-speaking north and a more racially mixed – eventually Anglicized – south. Largely English speaking, and less rugged than the north, the area south of the Landsker became known as 'Little England beyond Wales'. The difference is still evident today – in place names, church architecture and language.

Five of Pembrokeshire's best beaches

Barafundle, charming, sheltered cove, accessible from the coast path, page 54.
Broad Haven, magnificent stretch of sand with good facilities, page 52.
Marloes Sands, rugged and remote, with dramatic rock formations, page 52
Newgale, exposed to the Atlantic gales, great waves for watersports, page 52.
Whitesands, beautiful beach in a lovely setting with stunning walks, page 52.

Although coal and iron were mined in Pembrokeshire, today the main industries are agriculture and tourism. The **Pembrokeshire Coast National Park** was established in 1952 and is one of the smallest national parks, covering 232.5 sq miles (602 sq km), as well as the only one that is mainly coastal. The pristine beaches (13 are Blue Flag beaches) and clear seas are something close to heaven for watersports enthusiasts: surfers, windsurfers, kite surfers, sailors, kayakers – you name them, you'll find them here. You can even try coasteering, a mix of rock climbing, scrambling and swimming. The marine wildlife is thriving too, with huge colonies of puffins, kittiwakes, gannets and other seabirds on the islands, and dolphins, seals and porpoises easily spotted in the sea.

Newport (Trefdraeth) and around → *For listings, see pages 57-61.*

Lovely little Newport makes a great base for exploring the northern part of Pembrokeshire. The town's small streets, which stretch either side of the A487, provide easy pedestrian access to the Pembrokeshire Coast Path to the north. Head south and you can walk up the distinctive, brooding hill known as **Carn Ingli** – or 'Hill of Angels' – which was once topped with an Iron Age hillfort. You can still see the outlines of 25 ancient houses; archaeologists think around 150 people may have once lived here. The views from the top are great. There are more reminders of Newport's prehistoric past at **Carreg Coeltan** ⓘ *daily 1000-1600, free*, a Neolithic burial chamber reached via Feidr Pen-y-Bont road. Inevitably it was once claimed to be the burial spot of King Arthur. The TIC has plenty of information on walks and cycle routes in the area.

Nevern

Around two miles east of Newport is the little village of **Nevern**, site of the fascinating church of St Brynach, which was founded in the sixth century. Dark yew trees line the path, one of which (the second on the right) is known as the 'bleeding yew' on account of the reddish sap that oozes from it. Legend has it that a man was hanged from the tree for stealing a church plate. The churchyard is older than the church and beside the porch is an ancient stone known as the **Vitalianus Stone**, a fifth-century stone inscribed both in Latin and in Ogham (an Irish branch of Celtic then used in parts of Wales) and commemorating a British chieftain, or a Briton who served in the Roman army. The churchyard also contains the **Great Cross**, a 13-ft-high Celtic Cross, probably carved in the 10th century. Inside the church is another bilingual stone, the Maglocunus Stone and a Celtic carved Cross Stone. From the church you can bear right and uphill to visit **Pentre Ifan**, a vast Neolithic burial chamber that is probably one of the finest in Wales.

Unclassified roads that stretch between Nevern and Cardigan bring you to hidden sections of stunning coastline. Head for Moylegrove and you can get to **Ceibwr Bay**, where you can walk a section of the coastal path or simply gaze at the dramatic cliffs and swooping sea birds. Further north, a little road leads from St Dogmaels to the lovely beach at **Poppit Sands**, then to a tranquil estuary and the headland of **Cemaes Head**.

Castell Henllys

Four miles east of Newport, just off the A487, is **Castell Henllys** ⓘ *T01239-891319, Easter to end Oct daily 1000-1700, guided tours take place twice a day, £4.75, concessions £3.50, family £12.75*, a fascinating reconstructed Iron Age village, built on the site of an original hillfort. A footpath through the woods takes you to the circle of thatched roundhouses, where smoking fires burn and informed staff give demonstrations of weaving and other crafts. There are plenty of activities, especially during the school summer holidays. This was a working archeological site until 2008 and artefacts that were discovered are on display in the education centre – it's a great place for both children and adults.

Gwaun Valley (Cwm Gwaun)

This must be one of the least explored areas of Pembrokeshire and there's a lovely 'land that time forgot' feel to it; things change so slowly here that they still celebrate New Year (or Hen Galan) on 13 January, which is according to the ancient Julian calendar instead of the new fangled Gregorian one.

The Gwaun Valley is easily reached if you take the A487 from Newport towards Cardigan, and turn first right after the **Golden Lion** pub. A couple of miles further on there's a T-junction, where you turn right again and into the heart of this deep, wooded valley. Part way along you can turn off to visit lovely **Penlan-Uchaf Gardens** ⓘ *T01348-881388, www.penlan-uchaf.co.uk, Easter-Nov 0900-dusk*, where there are three acres of award-winning landscaped grounds with views to die for – it's a great spot for tea and home-made cake too. Further along is exquisite **Pontfaen Church** – a real ecclesiastical treasure. The church was founded in AD 540 but, after the Dissolution, was neglected and was almost ruined by the 19th century. However, it was later lovingly restored. In the churchyard are two pre-Conquest Latin crosses, while inside is a glistening icon painted by an Italian in 1902 – it's a copy of '*The Tabernacle of the Madonna of the Stars*' by Fra Angelico. On the road near the church is the blue-painted, and wonderfully time-warped, **Dyffryn Arms** (see Pubs, page 60).

Shortly after this you can take the B4313 left, to reach the eccentric village of **Rosebush**. It was once a slate-mining village but when the railway arrived the Victorian owners tried to turn it into a spa resort. Buildings were erected quickly in corrugated iron, but the visitors stayed away. The residents of this frontier-style settlement remained and it feels as if little has changed in the intervening years. The proposed hotel became a pub – the **Tafarn Sinc** or **Zinc Inn** (see Pubs, page 60). It's full of atmosphere and the name is a reference to the fact it's made of corrugated iron. Outside is what remains of the railway station; the last train ran in 1949. Close to Rosebush is **Pant Mawr farm shop** ⓘ *T01437-532627*, which sells local, artisan cheeses.

Fishguard (Abergwaun) and around → *For listings, see pages 57-61.*

Fishguard is rarely regarded as anything more than a stop-off to and from the nearby ferry port serving Ireland. However, its Lower Town was used extensively as a film location when Richard Burton made *Under Milk Wood* in the early 1970s and it attracts its fair share of Dylan Thomas fans. The town was also the location of one of Wales's most remarkable and historic battle victories. In 1797 an army of local women forced the surrender of French troops, the last invading army to land on the British mainland. Having arrived nearby at Carreg Wastad, legend has it that the invading troops mistook the traditional Welsh dress (black stovepipe hats and red flannel dresses) of the local women marching towards them for the outfit of British soldiers and instantly capitulated. One woman, pitchfork-wielding Jemima Nicholas, a 47-year-old cobbler, is known to have single-handedly captured 14 of the French soldiers; she is buried in the local church. The **Fishguard Tapestry** depicting this episode is on display in a purpose-built gallery in the library, upstairs in the Old Town Hall. A weekly produce market is held downstairs every Saturday morning.

Halfway along the seafront is **OceanLab** ⓘ *Goodwick (check for hours)*, which features an exhibition gallery about sea and shore life and has displays of fossils. Other facilities include a cyber café, soft play area for young children and coffee shop.

Fishguard to St David's

The stretch of coast between Fishguard and St David's is less commercialized than in the south and is better known for its rugged beauty and ancient landscape dotted with interesting little villages and beaches. For walkers, this stretch of the Pembrokeshire Coast Path (see box, page 46) is one of the most beautiful and remote; the path winds its way precariously over the cliffs, with secret coves tucked away beneath.

To the west of Fishguard, **Strumble Head**, with its lighthouse, is a good place for walking or for spotting migrating birds, seals, dolphins and even whales. Further down the coast, **Abercastell** is a tiny but charming fishing village with a few houses and a pub. The village's claim to fame is that in 1876 the first man to sail solo across the Atlantic in a fishing dory, landed here. Half a mile west of the village, just off the coastal path is **Carreg Samson** – a fine example of a Bronze Age burial chamber. Further south, you come to **Trefin**, the largest village on this stretch of coast. The nearby beach is easily accessible and, near the shore, stands the ruin of **Trefin Mill**, abandoned in 1918 but immortalized in the famous Welsh poem by William Williams, *Melin Trefin*. Perhaps the loveliest village is nearby **Porthgain**, with its ivy-covered remains of its former brickworks. It boasts a lively community, an attractive harbour and a great pub, **The Sloop Inn** (see Restaurants, page 59). The village grew to prominence in the mid-19th century as the port of export for slate and granite mined at nearby **Abereiddy**; the stretch of coast between the two is one of the most beautiful.

St David's (Tyddewi) and around → *For listings, see pages 57-61.*

No visit to Pembrokeshire is complete without a trip to St David's, Britain's smallest city famed for its magnificent cathedral, founded in AD 550 by St David, who was born and baptized nearby. The city is the most important religious site in Wales and has been a place of pilgrimage since the sixth century attracting saints, sinners and sightseers. Although it gets extremely busy, it somehow never loses its air of tranquillity. It's a lovely place to stay, with plenty of decent accommodation, and some good pubs and restaurants.

St David's Cathedral ⓘ *T01437-720199, www.stdavidscathedral.org.uk, daily 0900-1730, donations welcome, guided tours available in summer, or can be booked on T01437-720202*, is one of the oldest in Britain. It is built on the spot St David selected for his monastery, an area known as *Glyn Rhosyn* in Welsh, meaning 'valley of the little marsh'; it would have been a wild, deserted spot but well hidden from raiders. Early pilgrims included William the Conqueror, who came here in 1081, and Henry II who visited twice in 1171 and 1172. You can still see the restored shrine of St David. Set in its own grassy hollow on the edge of the city, the cathedral is a delightful place to explore, with lots of tombs, statues and ornate carvings to examine.

The building you see today dates back to the late 12th century, although there were many later additions and alterations – an earthquake damaged the building around 1247 and the floor of the nave has a discernible slope. As you enter you are struck by the fine carved ceiling, made of Irish oak. It was built in the late 15th century to conceal restoration work, when the building looked in danger of collapse again. If you look carefully you can see several Green Men carved here – the attendants can help you spot them – they are an ancient pagan symbol, thought to be associated with fertility and harvest, but considered by some to represent evil. The carved misericords in the choir are also worth a look, and include a particularly vivid depiction of a man being sick over the side of a boat. The choir contains a stall reserved for the monarch, unique in Britain – the queen being an automatic canon of the cathedral. Behind the choir, the presbytery has a brilliantly coloured 15th-century ceiling, which was restored and repainted in the 19th century by Sir George Gilbert Scott.

Close to the cathedral is the **Bishop's Palace** ⓘ *T01437-720517, Mar-Jun, Sep-Oct daily 0930-1700; Jul, Aug daily 0930-1800; Nov-Mar Mon-Sat 1000-1600, Sun 1100-1600, £3.20, concessions £2.80, family £9.20, CADW*, a magnificent ruin, built between 1328-1347 by Bishop Henry de Gower, who pulled out all the architectural stops to create a building that reflected the power and wealth of the church – and the bishop. You can see the remains of many of the fine carvings, ornate windows and grand state rooms, and there is also an exhibition on the life of the palace.

St David's Peninsula

This is a good place for walking, with inlets and coves around every corner. The peninsula is also served by the **Coastal Coaster** bus (see page 45). From the city you can walk south to the beach at **Caerfai** where the purple sandstone cliffs were quarried to provide masonry for St David's Cathedral. Just west of here is **St Non's Bay**, the spot at which St Non was said to have given birth to David – a spring suddenly appearing in the ground

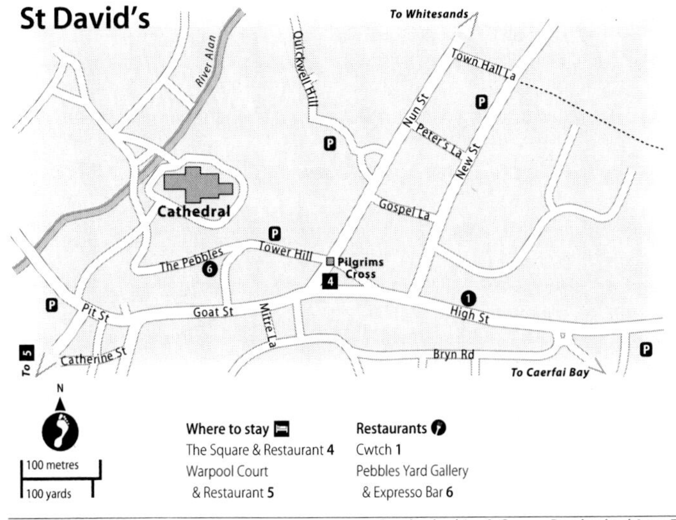

Where to stay
The Square & Restaurant **4**
Warpool Court & Restaurant **5**

Restaurants
Cwtch **1**
Pebbles Yard Gallery & Expresso Bar **6**

when he was born. There's a shrine here that still attracts pilgrims and the ruins of a 13th-century chapel, as well as a 20th-century chapel. Further round is the picturesque inlet of **Porthclais**, which was the port of the monastic community of St David's and supposedly the place where St David was baptized. Due west of St David's is the little harbour of **St Justinians** from where boats leave for **Ramsey Island** (see What to do, page 61), noted for its rich bird life, while the waters are great for spotting seals, whales and dolphins. Perhaps the most stunning beach on the peninsula, a couple of miles northwest of St David's, **Whitesands Bay** ⓘ *May-Sep, charge for car park, no dogs*, is a clean, sandy stretch popular with surfers and windsurfers, with a couple of campsites nearby. If you follow the Coast Path north from here, you reach the small, secluded beach at **Porthmelgan**.

St Bride's Bay and the islands → *For listings, see pages 57-61.*

To the south of St David's, the Coast Path takes you round the curve of St Bride's Bay, past some stunning scenery with plenty of camping and caravanning spots. The first place you come to is the picturesque little village of **Solva**, a beautiful rocky inlet providing a natural harbour for yachts and pleasure boats. In the 19th century it was a busy port where passenger services left for New York; today it has a number of little shops, art galleries and several good places to eat. Further round the bay are the endless sands of **Newgale** beach, fully exposed to the Atlantic winds, it is the longest beach on the bay and an excellent spot for all sorts of watersports. Further south, the lively holiday village of **Broad Haven** has a magnificent beach and some interesting rock formations while, tucked away nextdoor, **Little Haven** has a small attractive sandy cove and craggy harbour and is one of the centres for scuba diving in the area. Out on the southern peninsula, there is a glorious clifftop walk, accessible from the National Trust car park (charge) at **Marloes**, from where you can reach the quieter sandy beach of **Marloes Sands**. The village of **Dale** is a popular watersports centre while **Martins Haven**, near Marloes, is the usual starting point for trips to the islands of Skomer, Skokholm and Grassholm (see below).

Skomer, Skokholm and Grassholm islands

These offshore islands are nature reserves famed for their huge population of seabirds in the spring and summer months. The boats usually run from April to October, weather permitting. Contact the **Wildlife Trust for South and West Wales (WTSWW)** ⓘ *T01239-621600, www.welshwildlife.org*, or **Dale Sailing Company** ⓘ *T01646-603110, www.dale-sailing.co.uk*, for details. The visitor 'gateway' to the islands is **Lockley Lodge**, Martin's Haven, near Marloes.

Skomer is home to one of the most the most easily accessible of all seabird colonies in northwest Europe, and has been a National Nature Reserve (NNR) since 1959. Puffins and Manx shearwaters are the island's most famous residents, to be seen throughout the summer until August. There is a huge range of other wildlife including grey seals, which pup between September and November, the common porpoise and dolphins. The island also contains the remains of Iron Age huts and ancient field systems. To the south is **Skokholm**. Walkers may enjoy boat trips in the summer around this WTSWW reserve to view the puffins, Manx shearwaters and storm petrels up close. Some 11 miles off the coast, and the smallest of the three islands, is **Grassholm**, an RSPB reserve housing 35,000 breeding pairs of gannets. These give rise to the island's nickname the 'Wedding Cake' as, from a distance, it appears to be covered in a white icing. Landing is not allowed but boat trips can take you close to the island.

Haverfordwest (Hwlffordd) and around → *For listings, see pages 57-61.*

The main transport hub and shopping centre of Pembrokeshire, Haverfordwest offers little in the way of tourist attractions, though there's a ruined castle and small museum and art gallery. The 12th-century castle was the focus around which the town developed, later becoming a prosperous port in the 17th and 18th centuries. If you head three miles east of the town, off the A40, you'll find **Picton Castle and Woodland Gardens** ⓘ *The Rhos, T01437-751326, www.pictoncastle.co.uk, Apr-Sep daily 1030-1700, £9.50, children £5, family £24.50, guided tours of castle 1215-1415; gardens and gallery only £6.50, children £4*, a 13th-century castle set in 40 acres of beautiful grounds, including woodlands, ferns, a maze and a walled garden. The Walled Garden contains a large collection of culinary and medicinal herbs.

Scolton Manor Museum and Country Park ⓘ *Spittal, off B4329 4 miles northeast of Haverfordwest; Museum T01437-731328, Easter-Oct daily 1030-1730; Park, T01437-731457 Apr-Oct 0900-1800, Nov-Mar 0900-1630; charge*, is an early Victorian manor house set in 60 acres of grounds, with a nature reserve. The museum concentrates on the history and natural history of Pembrokeshire and there are period furnished rooms in the house. There's a visitor centre, country trails, picnic sites and play areas.

Narbeth (Arbeth)

The town of Narberth lies at the hub of the Landsker Borderlands. It was one of the homes of the Princes of Dyfed and is even mentioned in the *Mabinogion*, an early collection of Welsh folk tales. Among the art studios in town is the **Creative Café** ⓘ *Spring Gardens, Narberth T01834-861651, www.thecreativecafe.co.uk, Easter-Oct daily 1000-1730*, a studio/café with a difference. Kids can enjoy painting designs on ready-made pottery, leave it to be glazed and collect in a couple of days (postal service available). There's also a coffeeshop.

Oakwood Park

Just to the west of Narbeth is **Oakwood Park** ⓘ *Canaston Bridge, T01834-815170, www.oakwoodthemepark.co.uk, usually Easter-Sep 1000-1700, Jul-Aug until 2200 but hours vary so check beforehand, £21 age 13+, £15 age 3-12, from £66 family*, Wales' answer to Alton Towers. Oakwood has a watercoaster, sky-coaster and large wooden rollercoaster. **CC2000**, Oakwood's indoor family entertainment centre, is an all-weather complex including a Crystal Maze and a 10-pin bowling alley; a log flume ride is due to open in 2013. A new attraction right next door to Oakwood is the **Blue Lagoon**, an indoor waterworld with waves, flumes and a lazy river. It's open all year.

Pembroke (Penfro) and around → *For listings, see pages 57-61.*

On Pembrokeshire's south coast is the pleasant, but rather uninspiring, market town of Pembroke, which developed after the building of a castle here in 1093 – the mightiest of the Norman castles in the south west of Wales. The heart of the town is the Main Street, an attractive jumble of Georgian and Victorian buildings that runs down from the fine castle – undoubtedly the main reason for visiting.

Pembroke Castle ⓘ *T01646-684585, www.pembroke-castle.co.uk, daily Apr to end Aug 0930-1800, Mar, Sep, Oct 1000-1700, Nov-Feb 1000-1600, £5.50, concessions £4.50, family £16*, was first built in 1093 by Roger de Montgomery, cousin of William the Conqueror. The original building was made of timber, but was strong enough to withstand a long siege from the Welsh. In 1204 work began to reconstruct the castle in stone, a task finished

St Govan's Chapel

One of the most striking sights here is St Govan's Chapel, a tiny chapel squeezed into a cleft in the rocks. It's thought to be 13th century but could be earlier. St Govan, an Irish monk, was said to have been visiting Pembroke when he was attacked by pirates. The rock is said to have miraculously unfolded allowing him to hide. He spent many years living in this remote spot and is meant to be buried under the altar. A well here was said to offer miraculous cures for eye complaints and rheumatism. You can visit the chapel by a long stairway, but access is sometimes limited because it is within military grounds. Ask at the local TIC or ring T01646-662367.

around 1247. In 1452 Jasper Tudor was granted the castle, and in 1457 his nephew, the future Henry VII and first Tudor king, was born here. During the Civil War the castle withstood another long siege, until the garrison surrendered – after which much of the building was destroyed on Cromwell's orders. Today the ruins you see have been restored. There's a Keep or Great Tower, a Norman Hall, dating from c1150-1170, and a spiral staircase leading to **Wogan's Cavern**, an unexpectedly large, dank cave that was used as a shelter as far back as the Palaeolithic Period, and continued intermittently into the Mesolithic age. There are re-enactments of historical events every weekend in the summer holidays and a café on site.

Pembroke to Tenby

South of Pembroke is a gloriously unspoiled coastline. The Stackpole Estate is owned by the National Trust and encompasses sheer cliffs and quiet beaches. **Stackpole Quay**, a tiny natural harbour, has a good tearoom (see Restaurants, page 59) and is a good starting point for walks on the cliffs. From here you can follow an easy path for half a mile over the clifftops to **Barafundle Bay**, a lovely stretch of sand and dunes. Footpaths continue to Stackpole Head, Broad Haven South and Bosherston – where the rugged offshore rock formation known as **Stack Rocks** teems with birdlife, including a large colony of guillemots. Just inland, near Bosherston, are **Bosherston Lily Ponds**, a series of man-made lakes created in the late 18th and early 19th centuries. They now support a range of wildlife, including otters, toads and kingfishers. Further west the land is owned by the MOD, within which lies the enigmatic **St Govan's Chapel**, tucked away in the cliffs (see box, above). At the tip of the peninsula is **Freshwater West** beach, known to have the most consistent surf in Wales. It also featured in *Harry Potter and the Deathly Hallows*, though the Shell Cottage is no longer there. A little further west is the lovely little village of Angle. The **Coastal Cruiser** bus service runs between Pembroke and Angle, Freshwater West, Stack Rocks, Broadhaven, Stackpole and Lamphey.

The A4139 south east of Pembroke takes you first to the ruined **Bishop's Palace** ⓘ *(CADW), Lamphey, T01646-672224, Mar-Oct daily 1000-1700, £3.20, concessions £2.80, family £9; Nov-Mar 1000-1600 free*. This was the country retreat of the bishops of St David's and has everything from fishponds to orchards. Further along the road you come to a turning for Manorbier, where there's a lovely ruined castle overlooking a sandy beach. **Manorbier Castle** ⓘ *Bus No 349, T01834-871317, www.manorbiercastle.co.uk, Easter to end Sep 1000-1800, £5, children £3*, was the birthplace in 1146 of Giraldus Cambrensis, or Gerald of Wales, the medieval churchman who travelled widely through Wales and chronicled the country and its people.

Wales and film

The Hollywood actor Ioan Gruffudd hails from Cardiff, and Catherine Zeta Jones from nearby Mumbles; then there's the renowned Sir Anthony Hopkins, as well as Rhys Ifans and Matthew Rhys. With big names like that, it's not surprising that Wales has an increasingly fertile film scene. There's an excellent film school situated at Caerleon, near Newport, and Dragon Studios, a state-of-the-art film studio complex, are located near Bridgend. Some films are set in Wales, such as the cult film *Human Traffic* (1999), which was set in Cardiff. Welsh locations have long been used as a dramatic backdrop: the sand dunes of Merthyr Mawr in *Lawrence of Arabia* (1962); Raglan Castle in *Time Bandits* (1981); Caerphilly Castle in *Restoration* (1995), Snowdonia in the second *Tombraider* (2003). A number of big-budget Bollywood films have also been shot at locations in Cardiff, Caerphilly and the Brecon Beacons. The Brecons also featured in *King Arthur* (2004) which starred Keira Knightley, and Ioan Gruffudd as heroic Sir Lancelot, and in *Killer Elite* (2011) with Clive Owen and Robert De Niro. *The Libertine* (2005), a period romp starring Johnny Depp was shot at Tretower Court and Castle. Pembrokeshire's beautiful beaches are an enduring favourite with filmmakers: Marloes Sands was used in *Snow White and the Huntsman* (2012) with Charlize Theron, while Freshwater West was a location for Ridley Scott's *Robin Hood* (2010), and also featured in *Harry Potter and the Deathly Hallows* Parts 1 and 2 (2010/2011).

East of Pembroke, off the A477, is **Carew Castle and Tidal Mill** ⓘ *T01646-651782, daily end Mar to Oct 1000-1700, £4.75, children £3.50, family £12.75.* The castle was built by the Normans but altered and extended over the years, eventually becoming an Elizabethan country mansion. It's now ruined but is often used as the setting for events in summer. The Tidal Mill was built in the 19th-century and was powered, as the name suggests, by the force of the tides. It is one of only three in Britain, and retains the original machinery.

Tenby (Dinbych y Pysgod) and around → *For listings, see pages 57-61.*

Tenby must qualify as one of the most delightful seaside towns in Britain. Perched on a rocky promontory above endless sandy beaches, with a fringe of pastel-coloured buildings set around a cosy harbour, it has a genteel, but lively, charm. The town's mix of award-winning beaches, winding medieval streets, and busy bars and restaurants allow it to appeal to a wide range of people, whether young surfers, city slickers on a weekend break or families on holiday. It's also an important stop on the Pembrokeshire Coast Path, and there's plenty of accommodation for weary walkers.

The town's Welsh name means 'Little Fort of Fishes'. It grew up around the Norman castle, first mentioned in records in 1153, the remains of which are perched on the headland. In the 13th century the town was partly enclosed by protective walls, which were later extended and strengthened. Tenby gradually developed into a thriving port and, although trade declined during the Civil Wars, enjoyed a revival in the 18th century as a salt water spa. The arrival of the railway in the 19th century attracted large numbers of visitors keen to enjoy the health-giving benefits of the seaside. It became a fashionable Victorian resort and attracted a wide range of people, from the naturalist PH Gosse to artists and authors such as Lewis Carroll, George Elliot and JMW Turner.

In the heart of the town is **St Mary's Church**, with its 152-ft spire. Among those commemorated is Robert Recorde, a mathematician born in Tenby circa 1510, who was said to have invented the 'equals' sign. On Quay Hill is the **Tudor Merchant's** ⓘ *(National Trust), T01834-842279, Easter-Oct Mon-Fri, Sun 1100-1700, £3.40, children £1.70, family £8.50*, one of the oldest buildings in town dating back to the 15th century. A former wealthy merchant's house, it is on three floors. You can see the remains of 18th-century seccos on the walls (they're like frescoes but painted onto dry rather than wet plaster) and see how the family would have lived. It was a family home until 1915 so there's plenty of atmosphere.

In the remains of the castle is the **Museum and Art Gallery** ⓘ *T01834-842809, www.tenbymuseum.org.uk, daily 1000-1700 (closed Sun, Mon in winter), £4*. This includes exhibits on the town's geology, maritime and social history, and has a permanent art collection which includes works by locally bred artists Augustus and Gwen John and Nina Hamnett.

To the east of Tenby is the pleasant village of **Amroth**, with its sheltered, south-facing beach. It's the end (or start) of the **Pembrokeshire Coast Path** (see box, page 46).

Tenby

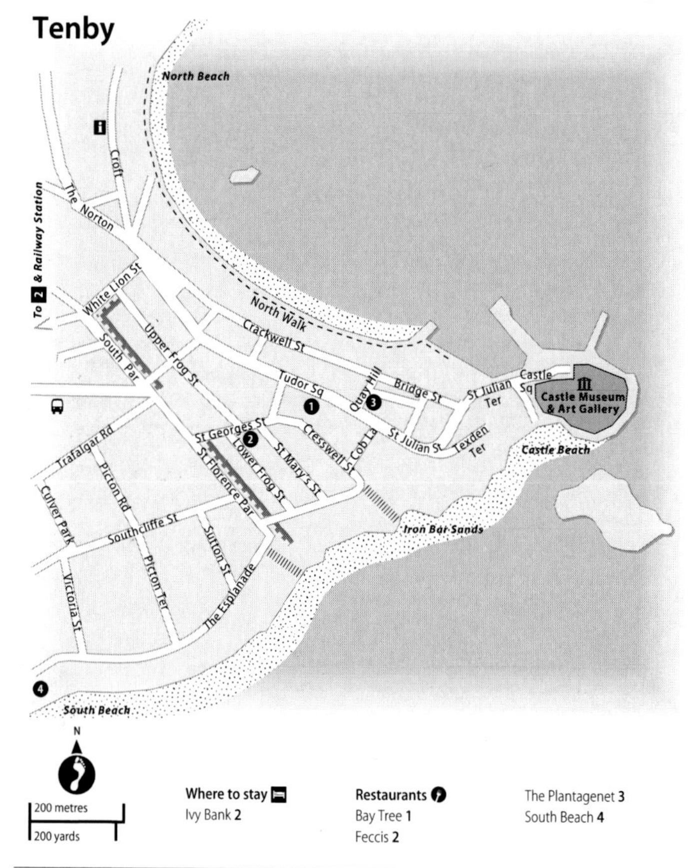

Where to stay
Ivy Bank **2**

Restaurants
Bay Tree **1**
Feccis **2**
The Plantagenet **3**
South Beach **4**

Further east is the sandy beach of **Wiseman's Bridge**, which was used for the D-Day rehearsals in 1944, supervised by Sir Winston Churchill himself. At low tide it is possible to walk along the beach all the way to neighbouring **Saundersfoot**, one of the area's most popular family resorts.

Caldey Island

Caldey Island, just a few miles south of the mainland, has been a monastic settlement since around the sixth century and is now a popular destination for **boat trips** ⓘ *T01834-844453, www.caldey-island.co.uk, Easter-Oct Mon-Sat, charge*, from Tenby. In the early Middle Ages a Benedictine order founded a priory here, but it was deserted after the Dissolution. The island is now home to a small community of monks of the Reformed Cistercian Order, who manufacture a range of products including perfumes and toiletries inspired by the island's wild flowers, gorse and herbs. The abbey church is open, and there's a little museum and tea garden on the island.

Pembrokeshire listings

For hotel and restaurant price codes and other relevant information, see pages 15-19.

Where to stay

Newport and around *p48*

££££-£££ Llysmeddyg, East St, T01239-820008, www.llysmeddyg.com. Lovely large, airy rooms in this clean and stylish restaurant with rooms. Breakfast from local and organic foods, with imaginative veggie options.

£££ Gellifawr Hotel and Cottages, Pontfaen, Gwaun Valley, T01239-820343, www.gellifawr.co.uk. Lovingly restored 19th-century stone farmhouse and cottages in a tranquil setting. Comfortably furnished, spacious rooms. Friendly bar and excellent restaurant.

££ Cnapan, East St, T01239-820575, www.cnapan.co.uk. Well-established, popular 4-star restaurant with rooms set in an elegant Georgian townhouse.

Self-catering

Tregynon Country Cottages, Gwaun Valley, T01239-820531, www.tregynon-cottages.co.uk. Award-winning self-catering cottages, with great views of the Gwaun Valley. Wonderful base for walking.

Fishguard and around *p49*

£££-££ Fishguard Bay Hotel, Quay Rd, Goodwick, T01348-873571, www.fishguardbayhotel.co.uk. Originally a mansion converted to accommodate passengers on the mail steamers to Ireland, this renovated grande dame of an hotel is comfortable and rather old-fashioned in its faded elegance and the views of Fishguard Bay are stunning – worth booking a sea view.

££ Glanmoy Lodge Guesthouse, Tref-Wrgi Rd, Goodwick, T01348-874333, www.glanmoylodge.co.uk. 10 mins' walk from the port, comfortable and clean en suite rooms in a secluded location. There's even a chance to watch badgers at night.

££ Ivy Bridge Guesthouse, Drim Mill, Dyffryn, Goodwick, T01348-875366, www.ivybridgefishguard.co.uk. Popular B&B with an indoor swimming pool. Evening meals if required. Walkers and cyclists welcome.

Camping

Fishguard Bay Caravan and Camping Park, Garn Gelli, Fishguard, T01348-811415, www.fishguardbay.com. Mar-Dec.

St David's and around *p50, map p51*

££££ Warpool Court Hotel, T01437-720300, www.warpoolcourthotel.com. Pay the extra for a sea view if you can, at this comfortable, friendly hotel on the edge of town. Relaxing gardens, swimming pool, tennis court and 3000 exquisite hand-painted tiles dotted all over the hotel.

££££-£££ Crug-Glas Country House, near Abereiddy, T01348-831302, www.crug-glas.co.uk. A large working farm with 5-star accommodation. Rooms are carefully designed and comfortable with en suite bathrooms. Dinner and afternoon tea available. It's a luxurious base for exploring the coast. Book early as it's very popular.

££ The Square, Cross Sq, T01437-720333, www.square-gallery.co.uk. Closed Jan and Feb. Small but cool accommodation above an art gallery, with stripped wooden floors, sleek chrome fittings and lush pot plants. Egyptian cotton sheets on the beds and tasty breakfasts. There's just 1 double room and 1 tiny single.

Self-catering

Trevaccoon, Llanrhian, near St David's, T01348-837797, www.trevaccoon.co.uk. 4-star self-catering cottages on a 4-acre country estate.

Camping

Campsites in the area include:

£ Caerfai Farm Camp Site, close to Caerfai Bay, T01437-720274, www.caerfaibay.co.uk. May-Sep. Toilets and showers.

£ Newgale Camp Site, Wood Farm, Newgale, T01437 710253, www.newgalecampingsite.co.uk. Easter-Oct. Camp in the field just across the road from gorgeous Newgale beach.

Haverfordwest and around *p53*

£££ Wolfcastle Country Hotel, Wolfcastle, near Haverfordwest, T08719-958290, www.wolfcastle.com. Recently refurbished hotel, well placed for exploring St David's or the Preseli Hills. The restaurant's noted for its fresh fish dishes.

££ Lower Haythog Farm, Spittal, near Haverfordwest, T01437-731279, www.lowerhaythogfarm.co.uk. Cosy dairy farm with clean, comfortable rooms and great farmhouse breakfasts.

Narberth and around *p53*

££££ The Grove, Molleston, near Narberth, T01834-860915, www.thegrove-narberth.co.uk. Beautifully restored country house set in its own grounds, with elegant and stylish accommodation. Some rooms are in a 15th-century Welsh longhouse, others in the main property. The restaurant serves modern British food.

Self-catering

Bluestone, Canaston Wood, near Narberth, T01834-862400, www.bluestonewales.com. **Bluestone** is a high-quality holiday resort set in the national park. Accommodation is in timber lodges, cottages and studios in and around a 'village' centre. There are several restaurants, bars and cafés on site as well as food shops. A range of activities for families are available, as well as a spa for adults.

Pembroke and around *p53*

££££ Lamphey Court Hotel, Lamphey, T01646-672273, www.lampheycourt.co.uk. An imposing colonnaded mansion with good leisure facilities including an indoor pool, a spa and 2 tennis courts.

££ Portclew House, Freshwater East, T01646-672800, www.portclewhouse.co.uk. A listed Georgian building with large rooms, set in its own grounds. Self-catering cottages are also available.

££ Poyerston Farm, Cosheston, near Pembroke, T01646-651347, www.poyerstonfarm.co.uk. Lovely clean and comfortable rooms on this friendly working farm. Flowery fabrics and traditional touches throughout. Breakfast is taken in the conservatory.

££ Williams of Solva, 10 Main St, Solva, T01437-729000, www.williamsofsolva.co.uk. High-quality B&B in a Georgian house. Egyptian cotton sheets, en suite facilities and a good organic breakfast.

Tenby and around *p55, map p56*

££££ St Brides Hotel and Spa, St Brides Hill, Saundersfoot, near Tenby, T01834-812304, www.stbridesspahotel.com. Contemporary and stylish rooms, many of which have a sea view, make this hotel a great option for couples. The spa has an infinity pool and offers a range of relaxing treatments. It's only a 5-min drive from Tenby.

££££-£££ Penally Abbey, Penally, near Tenby, T0871-995 8254, www.penally-abbey.com. Secluded country house on the site of an ancient abbey, set in 12 acres of grounds. Lots of antiques and period furniture. Conveniently close to an 18-hole golf course.

££ Ivy Bank, Harding St, T01834-842311, www.ivybanktenby.co.uk. 4-star B&B in a Victorian house. All rooms are en suite and non-smoking.

££ Wychwood House, Penally, near Tenby, T01834-844387. 3 large, en suite rooms and lovely views at this attractive B&B.

Self-catering

For unusual self-catering cottages and gypsy caravans in the area, check out Under the Thatch, www.underthethatch.co.uk.

Restaurants

Newport and around *p48*

£££ Cnapan, East St, T01239-820575, www.cnapan.co.uk. There's a country house atmosphere at this well-established restaurant serving modern British dishes with a twist. Fresh local produce is used and they make their own bread. You might find Welsh beef, seafood chowder or spicy fish cakes on the menu. Plenty of choices for veggies too. Desserts include damson sorbet with sloe gin.

£££ Gellifawr, Pontfaen, Gwaun Valley, T01239-820343, www.gellifawr.co.uk. Excellent restaurant, with traditional stone and woodburning fire, serving à la carte and bistro meals using fresh local produce. Friendly and welcoming.

£££ Llysmeddyg, East St, T01239-820008, booking advised. Fresh seasonal and locally sourced produce. Dishes such as lamb rump with vanilla parsnips and greens. Veggie options available.

££-£ The Golden Lion, East St, T01239-820321, www.goldenlionpembrokeshire.co.uk. Popular pub serving good bar meals.

£ Old Post Office Tea Rooms, Rosebush, T01437-532205. Pretty little tea rooms tucked away behind the distinctive corrugated-iron buildings of Rosebush.

St David's and around *p50, map p51*

£££ Cwtch, 22 High St, St David's, T01437-720491, www.cwtchrestaurant.co.uk. Relaxed atmosphere and imaginative, locally sourced food. The menu might include smoked mackerel and lime fishcakes, and slow-roasted pork belly with onion gravy. Vegetarian choices too,

££ The Shed, Porthgain, T01348-831518, www.theshedporthgain.co.uk. Fish 'n' chips bistro using fresh fish caught by the owner.

££-£ The Sloop Inn, Porthgain, T01348-831449, www.sloop.co.uk. Dating back to 1743, this great inn serves a good range of bar meals, and pricier specials with lots of fresh fish and lamb shanks – around £13. There's a maritime theme inside with old ropes and floats. Serves real ales.

£ Pebbles Yard Gallery and Espresso Bar, The Pebbles, T01437-720122. Relaxed contemporary café above a gift shop, with outside seating area. Good for filled pitta breads, sandwiches, cakes and coffee.

Haverfordwest and around *p53*

£££ George's, 24 Market St, T01437-766683, www.thegeorges.uk.com. Established eaterie offering good-value cuisine, with dishes such as seafood chowder, Welsh fillet of beef or veggie crêpes.

Pembroke and around *p53*

£ Boathouse Tearoom, Stackpole Quay, T01646-672687. Lovely licensed tea room close to beautiful Barafundle Bay.

Home-made cakes, filled baguettes and jacket potatoes as well as imaginative dishes, such as tomato and chive tart with feta.
£ Rowlies, 2 Main St, T01646-686172. Award-winning fish and chips that you can take away or sit in and eat.

Tenby *p55, map p56*
££££ The Bay Tree, Tudor Sq, T01834-843516, www.baytreetenby.co.uk. One of the most popular places to eat, with a wide range of meat dishes and several veggie options.
£££ The Plantagenet, Quay Hill, Tudor Sq, T01834-842350, www.plantagenettenby.co.uk. Situated in an historic building in Tenby, this restaurant serves up local seafood, organic meat and freshly made vegetarian dishes.
£££-££ South Beach, Water's Edge, South Beach, T01834-843167/02920-782079, www.southbeachbargrill.com. A new bar and grill on the Tenby waterfront. Come for the relaxed atmosphere and to enjoy steaks, seafood and salads – as well as some veggie dishes.
£ Feccis, Upper Frog St. Well-established Italian ice cream parlour, where you can settle down to a huge knickerbocker glory, or buy a cone to slurp on the beach. Also has a fish and chip shop on Lower Frog St.

Pubs

Newport and around *p48*
Dyffryn Arms, Pontfaen. Fantastic old pub untouched by the 20th, let alone 21st century. Bessie, the landlady, whose family has owned it since 1845, serves beer poured into jugs from behind a serving hatch. Simple living room lined with seats and a real fire in winter.
Tafarn Sinc, Rosebush, T01437-532214. The red corrugated-iron exterior hides a great little pub inside, with sawdust on the floor, old settles and lots of old photos. Real ales.

Fishguard *p49*
Ship Inn, Newport Rd, Lower Town, Cluttered yet cosy, this rather eccentric little inn is a great place to while away the hours.

St David's and around *p50, map p51*
Druidston Hotel, Druidston, T01437-781221. A bohemian hotel and bar high up on the cliffs with great views.
Farmers Arms, Goat St, T01437-720328. The liveliest and most popular pub in St David's. Serves real ales and has a garden. Bar meals available lunchtimes and evenings.

Haverfordwest *p53*
The Fishguard Arms, Old Bridge Close, T01437-768123. Excellent food at reasonable prices and real ales in a friendly atmosphere, with live music (jazz, folk, soul) at weekends.
The Griffin Inn, Dale, T01646-636227, www.griffininndale.co.uk. This pub on the seafront at Dale offers real fires in winter, Welsh ales and great food.

Pembroke and around *p53*
The Watermans Arms, 2 The Green, T01646-682718. Situated just over the bridge, this pub has a veranda where you can sit and look over the water while enjoying a pint or one of their bar meals.

Festivals

May/early Jun St David's Cathedral Festival, T01437-720271, www.stdavidscathedral.org.uk. Annual classical music festival.
Aug Pembrokeshire County Show, County showground, Haverfordwest, T01437-764331. 3-day agricultural show in mid-Aug.
Sep Tenby Arts Festival, T01834-84229, www.tenbyartsfest.com. Annual week-long music and arts festival.

What to do

Boat trips

Thousand Islands Expeditions, Cross Sq, St David's, T01437-721721, www.thousandislands.co.uk. RSPB cruises to Ramsey Island wildlife reserve, with an opportunity to land on the island and see various sea birds. Also runs sea trips to watch basking sharks, pilot whales and dolphins.

Voyages of Discovery, 1 High St, St David's, T01437-721911, www.ramseyisland.co.uk. Whale and dolphin watching and tours of the coast.

Cycling

Mikes Bikes, 17 Prendergast, Haverfordwest, T01437-760068, www.mikes-bikes.co.uk. Mon-Sat. Cycle hire for all the family.

Newport Bike Hire, East St, Newport, T01239-820724, www.newportbikehire.com. Hire of a range of mountain bikes, children's bikes, helmets. Also have maps.

Diving

There are several diving centres/ schools in Pembrokeshire.

Celtic Diving, Main St, Goodwick, T07816-640684, www.celticdiving.co.uk. Courses in snorkelling, scuba and specialist skills. Wreck dives.

Dive Pembrokeshire, Peggys Cove, 11 Meadow Park, Burton, Milford Haven, T07748-971331/07545-967180, www.dive-pembrokeshire.com. Dive and powerboat courses.

Horse riding

East Nolton Riding Stables, Nolton, Haverfordwest, T01437-710360, www.noltonstables.com. Riding and trekking for all abilities, also has accommodation.

Outdoor activities

Sealyham Activity Centre, Wolfcastle, Haverfordwest, T01348-840763, www.sealyham.com. Runs courses from 1-5 days in kayaking, surfing, rock climbing, coasteering or dinghy sailing. Pre-booking needed.

Tyf Adventure, 1 High St, St David's, T01437-721611, www.tyf.com. Offers coasteering, surfing, kayaking and climbing. Taster sessions, ½ day, full day and longer programmes available.

Sailing

Solva Sailboats, 1 Maes-y-Forwen, Solva, T01437-720972, www.solva.net/solvasailboats. Sailing and powerboat courses.

Surfing

Ma Simes Surf Hut, 28 High St, St David's, T01437-720433, www.masimes.co.uk. Surf hire and surfing lessons, on Whitesands beach, also sells surfing kit.

Newsurf, Newgale, T01437-721398, www.newsurf.co.uk. Daily surf reports, hires out and sells surf skis, surfboards, body boards and wet suits, and also offers instruction.

Walking

See box on the Pembrokeshire Coast Path, page 46.

Transport

Ferry

Fishguard's ferry terminal is in **Goodwick** (Wdig) about a mile from the town centre and is served by rail and bus connections. **Stena Line** ferries (T0870-570 7070, www.stena line.com), operates 2 types of vessel between **Rosslare** in Ireland and **Fishguard**: a superferry completes the journey in about 3½ hrs. Buses usually meet ferries.

Pembroke Dock terminal (**Irish Ferries**). 2 ferries a day at 1345 and 1445. The nearest Station (Pembroke Dock) is about a mile from the terminal so allow sufficient time for a taxi to pick you up as there are unlikely to be any waiting at the station or terminal.

Ceredigion Coast

For most of its history Ceredigion was largely isolated from the rest of Wales by the Cambrian mountains. Consequently, the Welsh language, culture and sense of identity are still strong – though somewhat diluted by English settlers and visitors. The area was once an independent principality and takes its name from Prince Ceredig. Much of this beautiful area is designated Heritage Coast and is one of the best places to come to observe marine wildlife. It shelters some of Britain's rarest birds and is home to a resident population of bottlenose dolphins, as well as harbour porpoises and grey seals. The rivers and estuaries also provide superb wildlife habitats where you have the chance to spot wildfowl, rare plants and otters. Go further inland and you can see red kites which are fed daily. Many of the pretty seaside villages feel almost Cornish in character, such as Georgian Aberaeron and bustling New Quay – a favourite haunt of the poet Dylan Thomas.

Arriving on the Ceredigion Coast

Tourist information

New Quay TIC ⓘ *Church St, T01545-560865, newquaytic@ceredigion.gov.uk*. **Aberaeron TIC** ⓘ *The Quay, T01545-570602, aberaerontic@ceredigion.gov.uk*. **Cardigan TIC** ⓘ *Theatr Mwldan, Bath House Rd, T01239-613230, cardigantic@ceredigion.gov.uk*. More information on Ceredigion can be found at www.ceredigion.gov.uk, www.visitcardigan.com and www.caridganshirecoastandcountry.com. Cardigan Bay also has a conservation website, www.cardiganbaysac.org.uk.

Aberaeron and around → *For listings, see page 66.*

Aberaeron, situated on the west coast south of Aberystwyth, comes as something of a surprise in this most Welsh of areas, as it looks distinctly English. It's a neat, orderly Georgian planned town, built almost from scratch in the 19th century, with wide streets and houses painted in cheery colours, set around a pretty harbour. It was built by the Reverend Alban Gwynne, who spent his wife's considerable inheritance creating the village that was reportedly designed by John Nash. His intention was to create a new port for Mid Wales. Unlike other places on this stretch of coast, Aberaeron doesn't have a great beach, however the waterfront is pleasant and there are some good pubs.

About two miles away on the A482 is **Llanerchaeron** ⓘ *(National Trust), T01545-570200, hours vary, call or see www.nationaltrust.org.uk to check as house may be closed but farm and garden open, £6.45, children £3.27, family £16.18*, a Welsh 18th-century gentry estate, once common in the area. The house, also designed by John Nash, has been restored and is furnished in Edwardian style, with fascinating servants' quarters and a service courtyard with a dairy, laundry and brewery. The estate operates as a working organic farm.

New Quay (Cei Newydd)

There's a salty tang to New Quay – a little village squeezed, in picturesque Cornish fashion, around a harbour. Dylan Thomas often visited and drank in the pubs, even living here for a time during 1944-1945. It was here that he started work on *Under Milk Wood*, so the town has a good claim to be the fictional 'Llareggub' in the play (see also page 43). One of the pubs, The Black Lion, witnessed a fight between Thomas and William Killick, a friend who returned from war service to discover that his wife, Vera, had been using his army pay to support Thomas and Caitlin. Killick suspected some sexual shenanigans, and they argued. Killick then got a machine gun and hand grenade, went to Majoda, the house the Thomas family were renting, and fired. He was arrested and tried for attempted murder. He was acquitted and Thomas sensibly left New Quay soon after. You can pick up a good, free Dylan Thomas walking trail of the village in the tourist information centre. The village is very lively in summer, you can go on dolphin-watching boat trips to see the bottlenose dolphins that follow shoals of mackerel in the bay, and there are plenty of pubs and places to eat.

A couple of miles away is **New Quay Honey Farm** ⓘ *T01545-560822, www.thehoneyfarm.co.uk, Easter-Oct daily 1000-1730, shop also open outside this season, admission charge*, with a small but informative exhibition on the life of the honey bee. Glass cases allow you to see bees coming and going to a huge honeycomb, and there are panels explaining the different ways they communicate. There's also a great café open Easter to October.

South of New Quay

The coastline here takes on an even more Cornish character, with stunning beaches and hidden coves linked by a maze of narrow, high-banked lanes teeming with wild flowers. **Llangrannog** (parking charge in peak season) is a charming little village with a tiny beach, bustling old pub, café and shop selling surfing gear and buckets and spades.

Just south of here is **Penbryn Beach**, owned by the National Trust, where trails lead to the Corbalani stone burial site of a fifth-century chief. The next beach along is **Tresaith** (parking charge in field above), another unspoiled cove where a waterfall cascades down from the cliffs; just next door is the busier, more popular beach at **Aberporth**. The most beautiful and unspoiled spot along here is **Mwnt** (parking £1.50), a remote headland owned by the National Trust, with a secluded, sandy beach below, reached by steep steps. Mwnt was a stopping place for the bodies of saints being taken to Bardsey Island, their traditional burial ground, and was also on a pilgrims' route to St David's. There's a lonely little church, **Holy Cross Y Mwnt**, the oldest in Ceredigion. It's a 13th-century building, but built on much older foundations. If you go in you can see that a small window on the north side has been walled up. It's thought that this let lepers, and others forbidden from the building, to observe the service from outside.

Cardigan (Aberteifi) and around

→ *For listings, see page 66.*

With such a gorgeous coastline to explore you are unlikely to want to linger long in Cardigan, though it's pleasant enough. The town was once one of the principal ports on Wales' west coast, dating back to its pre-Norman days. It was an important embarkation point for emigration to North America and ships such as *The Active* and *The Albion* took many emigrants to New Brunswick, Canada and New York in the 1840s. The family of the architect Frank Lloyd Wright left Wales from here. The **castle**, built in 1093, was the site of the first competitive eisteddfod in 1176, but was later badly damaged in the Civil War. Henry Tudor stayed there on his march to Bosworth. The castle is not open to the public although there is a campaign to bring it into public ownership.

Outside the town, a short drive on the B4548 to Gwbert, is the **Cardigan Island Coastal Farm Park** ⓘ *T01239-623637, www.cardiganisland.com, mid-Mar to Oct, admission charge*, where you can walk (or take a tractor ride) to a viewing point to spot seals that breed in the caves below. There are various farmed animals here, such as wallabies, llamas, emus and ponies, some of which children can feed if they wish; special feed is for sale. There's also a café with seats looking out to sea, but no indoor seating, so not one for a rainy day.

Cardigan hosts an annual **Walking Festival** each October and is also a base for a number of walks in the Teifi Estuary. See www.tourism.ceredigion.gov.uk for details of local events.

Cenarth

The A484 from Cardigan leads to pretty, but supremely touristy, Cenarth. This little village is famed for its tumbling rapids and salmon leap (car park charge) and was first mentioned by a 12th-century traveller Gerald Cambrensis, who passed through the village recruiting for the crusades and wrote of salmon 'leaping as high as the tallest spear'. It was high on the Victorian's 'must see' list. You can also visit the **National Coracle Centre** ⓘ *T01239-710980, www.coraclecentre.co.uk, Easter-Oct daily1030-1730, admission charge*, which contains coracles (small round boats dating back to the ice age) from around the world. Cenarth was once a centre for coracle fishing. The centre is housed in a 17th-century flour mill, and you can still see the waterwheel. The village has a craftshop, several pubs and a tea shop.

Families with energy to burn off might wish to head to the **Cenarth Adventure Centre** ⓘ *Allt Y Gelli, T01559-371621, www.cenarth-paintball.co.uk, daily*, which offers a variety of adventure experiences. Archery (aged seven plus) costs £7.50 for 30 minutes; off road remote control buggies cost £6.50 for 25 minutes; paintball target shooting is £5.50 for 50 paintballs; and a woodland challenge course (aged 10 plus, minimum six people) will set you you back £17.99 for a half day.

About a 10-minute drive inland from Cardigan is **Caws Cenarth** ⓘ *T01239-701432, www.cawscenarth.co.uk, Mon-Sat 1000-1700*. This farmhouse, set in tranquil countryside, is home to Caws Cenarth cheese which you can purchase in the family's farm shop. Try and get there between 1130 and 1500, as then you'll be able to see the cheese being made.

Cilgerran and around

On a promontory above the Teifi, **Cilgerran Castle** ⓘ *(CADW), Apr-Oct daily 1000-1700, Nov-Mar daily 1000-1600, £3.50, concessions £2.65, family £10.50, free in winter*, is a romantic castle that inspired both JMW Turner and Richard Wilson. Probably built in 1100 the castle was thought to have been the home of Nest, the Welsh 'Helen of Troy'. A beautiful princess of Deheubarth, she was married to Gerald of Windsor but was abducted from the castle in 1108 by her second cousin Prince Owain. Her husband escaped down a privy waste pipe. She later became mistress to others, including Henry I. Today the castle's most striking features are two large towers, each four storeys high.

Just east of Cilgerran, tucked away off the A478, is one of the best places for wildlife watching – the Welsh Wildlife Centre at **Teifi Marshes Nature Reserve** ⓘ *Cilgerran, T01239-621600, www.welshwildlife.org, reserve open all year, visitor centre Apr-Oct 1030-*

Owain's Uprising

One of the most important figures in Welsh history is **Owain Glyndŵr** (c1349-c1416), who led a mighty rebellion against English rule. He was an unlikely rebel, a wealthy man descended from the Princes of Powys and Deheubarth, who was well educated, studied law in London and even served in the English army: a pillar of the establishment. His rebellion stemmed from a prosaic dispute with his neighbour in the borders – Lord Grey of Ruthin appropriated a piece of his land and the courts refused to back Glyndŵr, treating him with great lack of respect. Infuriated, in 1400 he attacked the town of Ruthin with hundreds of Welsh supporters. It sparked a national uprising, with Welshmen living in England rushing home to support the cause. He attacked more towns in the north and later that year proclaimed himself Prince of Wales. Henry IV retaliated, not only with force but also by introducing a range of draconian laws forbidding the Welsh from holding public office, taking arms or holding assemblies. Not surprisingly, this fuelled support for the rebellion and Glyndŵr went on to take many castles, including Harlech. In 1404 he held the first Welsh parliament in Machynlleth, made alliances with France and Scotland, and was crowned King of Wales. However, the following year, when he made incursions over the border, he was beaten back by troops led by the king's teenage son – the future Henry V. In 1408, Harlech was taken by the king's forces and Glyndŵr was forced into hiding. He fled into the wilds of Snowdonia, and after that no one knows what happened to him – although he is known to have died by 1417. Only a mound remains of his birthplace Sycharth Castle, near Llangedwyn, north of Welshpool, and no one knows where he is buried, but the Welsh will never forget his fight for freedom. See also History, page 71.

1700, shorter hours in winter, free, charge for parking. The reserve encompasses river, marshland and woods and has walking trails which give you the opportunity to spot (if you're lucky) their resident otters, the rare Cetti's warbler, 18 species of dragonfly and visitors such as sedge warblers and wildfowl. The visitor centre has a very good café (1030-1700) and you can also join guided walks or canoe or kayaking trips.

Further east, off the A484 and past Newcastle Emlyn, is the **National Woollen Museum** ⓘ *Dre-Fach Felindre, Llandysul, T02920-573070, www.museumwales.ac.uk, Apr-Sep daily 1000-1700, Oct-Mar Tue-Sat 1000-1700, free*. This area was once the centre of the woollen industry and the museum is housed in the restored Cambrian Mills. You can see the buildings and the old machinery where uniforms for First World War soldiers were made, as well as trying your hand at making woollen cloth.

Ceredigion Coast listings

For hotel and restaurant price codes and other relevant information, see pages 15-19.

Where to stay

Aberaeron *p62*

££££-£££ The Harbourmaster, Pen Cei, T01545-570755, www.harbour-master.com. Brilliant cool and contemporary rooms with great views of the harbour. There's a fresh seaside feel throughout, with white and aquamarine decor, fine white sheets and CD players.

£££ Arosfa, Cadwgan Place, T01545-570120, www.arosfaguesthouse.co.uk. 4-star guesthouse by the quay. Serves award-winning breakfasts.

New Quay and around *p63*

££ The Grange Country House, Pentregat, near Llangrannog, T01239-654121, www.grangecountryhouse.co.uk. Elegance all the way at this pink-painted Georgian house, set down a narrow track in its own grounds. Very clean and comfortable, lovely deep baths and good fresh food.

Self-catering

Neuadd Farm, Llwyndafydd, south of New Quay, T01545-560324, www.neuadd-farm-cottages.co.uk. 5-star self-catering cottages with swimming pool in the grounds. Cottages sleep from 2-6 people.

Cardigan and around *p63*

£££ The Ship, Tresaith, Cardigan, T01239-811816, www.shiptresaith.co.uk. 4 rooms at this seaside inn, furnished in unfussy style.

££ Tipi West, Blaenannerch, near Cardigan, T07813-672336, www.teepeewest.co.uk. 3 tipis accommodating up to 25 people all together. Sleep on air beds (bring your own sleeping bag) and sit round the camp fire at night. The tipis are insulated with coconut matting and close enough to Cardigan Bay to hear the waves when you're tucked up in bed.

Restaurants

Aberaeron *p62*

£££-££ The Cellar, 8 Market St, T01545-574666, www.thecellar-aberaeron.co.uk. Contemporary comfort food served at this restaurant in Aberaeron. Tapas served in the summer.

£ The Hive on the Quay, Cadwgan Place, T01545-570445, www.thehiveaberaeron.com. Famed for its delicious honey ice cream, this restaurant overlooking the water also serves pizzas, sharing platters and salads.

New Quay *p63*

££ The Hungry Trout, 2 South John St, T01545-560680, www.thehungrytrout.co.uk. Good restaurant by the harbour with lots of fish dishes – you might find Teifi sewin and swordfish on the regularly changing menu. Vegetarian choices also available.

£ Glasshouse Café at the Welsh Wildlife Centre, near Cilgerran, T01239-621600. Good views over the reserve in this café above the visitor centre. Serves, cakes and hot drinks, as well as hot meals.

Background

Contents

Footprint features

History

Prehistory

There is evidence of human settlement in Wales as far back as 250,000 BC when a human tooth was discovered at Pontnewydd in North Wales. It is thought that these ancient Neanderthal inhabitants lived in small groups as hunter-gatherers and made little impact on the area. By **Palaeolithic** times, man appeared to be establishing more significant settlements and the remains of a skeleton, christened the **Red Lady** (actually a man), discovered at Paviland Cave on the Gower, have been dated variously at 24,000 or 16,500 BC. **Mesolithic** peoples left little for archaeologists to find, but the Neolithic settlers who followed them left traces which can still be seen today. The **Neolithic** colonists, short, dark people, sometimes called Iberians, came from the Mediterranean area. They were the first farmers and established settled communities, clearing forests, constructing villages – and building circles of standing stones (henges) and vast burial chambers for their dead. The best known of these is Stonehenge in Wiltshire, made from bluestones hacked from the Preseli Hills in Pembrokeshire, but Wales is littered with such mysterious monuments including Pentre Ifan in Pembrokeshire and Bryn Celli Ddu in Anglesey.

The Neolithic period morphed gradually into the **Bronze Age**, with its use of metals to make implements and pots, and increasingly sophisticated social structures. Hillforts (defended villages) began to appear, then around 600 BC the **Celts** arrived.

The Celts

The Celts originally came from the area around the Rhine in Europe. A tall, fair people with sophisticated social structures, they made a huge impact. They were noted for their love of war and imposed their ways on the existing tribes of Britain very quickly. They used iron, rather than other metals, were artistically skilled and had distinctive religious beliefs – with their religious leaders, the **Druids**, enjoying huge power. Caesar wrote of Celtic society that there were 'only two classes of men who are of any account...the common people are treated almost as slaves ...the two privileged classes are the Druids and the Knights'. They also brought with them a new language which had two distinct strands: **Goidelic** (the basis of the Celtic languages in the Isle of Man, Scotland and Ireland) and **Brythonic** (the basis of Cornish and Welsh).

Celtic tribes established themselves throughout Wales: the Silures in the southeast, Ordovices in the northwest, Demetae in the southwest and Cornovii and Deceangli in the northeast. The Celts flourished until the arrival of the Romans, who first came to Britain in 55 BC, and finally conquered much of it in AD 43.

The Romans

The Celtic/British tribes continued to fight the Romans, notably Boudicca's Iceni in eastern England, who spread throughout the country. Tribal leader Caratacus (Caradog) moved west to organize resistance but it was hard, as the tribes here weren't as socially cohesive as in the south and east. The only uniformity was provided by the powerful Druids, whose stronghold was in Anglesey, described by Roman writer, Tacitus, as the place where young men from all over Europe were trained for the 'priesthood'. However, the rougher landscapes of the west helped keep the Romans at bay and it was not until after AD 75, when the massive fort was built at Caerleon (Isca), that they could be said to have conquered Wales.

The Romans built roads throughout Wales, linking important forts at Caernarfon (Segontium) and Carmarthen (Moriduum), and settled down for a long occupation. Gradually their sophisticated language and ways of living – and later their new Christian religion – started to influence local Celtic culture. Essentially a stable Romano/British culture emerged which ended with the decline of the Roman Empire.

The Dark Ages

As the Roman Empire floundered it became increasingly difficult to defend isolated areas such as the western parts of Wales. The long, exposed coastline meant that Wales was subject to raids from Ireland in the west, with further incursions from the Picts in the north and the Saxons in the south. By the end of the fourth century the Romans no longer ruled Wales. Britain became subject to increasing raids from warring **Teutonic** tribes who established themselves in the south and east of England. **Christianity**, which had only taken a tenuous hold through the Romans, returned to Wales during the fifth and sixth centuries, with the arrival of missionaries from Ireland. **Illtud** introduced the idea of Celtic monasticism and established a religious school at **Llantwit Major** in south Wales; in AD 500 his pupil **St David** founded St David's cathedral in Pembrokeshire.

Around the same time, Irish settlers (who spoke the Goidelic tongue) began moving into western parts of Wales, but were expelled from the north by **Cunedda**, leader of the Brythonic speaking Votadini (Gododdin) tribe. Well organized, they established themselves in north Wales and gradually spread as far south as the Teifi. They set up the royal house of **Gwynedd** and consolidated the Brythonic language in Wales. By the sixth century a distinctive **Welsh language** was evolving. Latin was used for formal affairs like legal matters, but everyday speech was Welsh. The earliest known example of written Welsh is on an eighth-century stone.

The Welsh coast was also subject to raids from **Vikings**, who left their stamp in place names such as Skomer. The tribes in the west, who saw themselves as **Cymry** (compatriots), became isolated. Wales – which had been given an obvious border in the late 700s when **King Offa** built the great earthwork Offa's Dyke, to delineate his Mercian territory – began to develop a distinct identity.

In AD 856 **Rhodri Mawr** (the Great) beat off the Vikings and created a largely unified Wales, although as the practice of primogeniture (first born male inherits) did not apply in Wales, inheritance squabbles meant it was never as stable as England. More Viking raids in the mid-ninth century served only to increase links with England for defensive reasons, but Rhodri's grandson **Hywel Dda** (the Good) became king of most of Wales. He was the first Welsh ruler known to issue his own coins and is also recognized as the codifier of **Welsh Law**. After his death, the country descended into anarchy, only coming together under the rule of **Gruffydd ap Llywelyn** – who even managed to grab some lands off Edward the Confessor – before being killed by his own people at the behest of Harold, Edward's successor.

The Norman Conquest

The first Norman castle in Wales was built in 1067 at **Chepstow** and the Normans gradually encroached on Welsh lands. By the end of the 11th century they had reached Pembroke in the south and other parts of Wales. Norman barons, the **Marcher Lords**, were installed in castles along the border so as to get control of as much land (and income) as possible. Welsh kings paid **homage** to the Normans, securing peace until William's death. William's son, William Rufus, made some incursions into Wales and the Marcher lords gradually helped to secure much of the country – although the northwest region of Gwynedd remained independent. There was much infighting and under **Owain Gwynedd**, operating from his power base at Aberffraw on Anglesey, Gwynedd began expanding its influence, sucking in weaker Welsh territories. **Llywelyn ap Iorwerth** (known as 'the Great') further extended Gwynedd and even managed to capture some Norman castles, until King John retaliated. Matters were complicated still more when Llywelyn, who wanted to achieve feudal overlordship over all Wales, consolidated his powerful position by marrying King John's daughter. He paid homage to the king and had to accept him as his heir, should his marriage not produce a son. Further struggles ensued, with Llywelyn gaining Welsh support for his demands for land and a degree of autonomy. He united with the barons who made King John sign the Magna Carta and, in essence, ruled most of Wales.

After he died, the infighting started again and the Normans pushed back into Wales until Llywelyn's grandson **Llywelyn ap Gruffyd** ('the Last') took control, managing to regain lost lands. In 1267 Henry III acknowledged his influence with the Treaty of Montgomery, in which Llywelyn recognized the English crown – and in turn was recognized as '**Prince of Wales**'. Llywelyn consolidated his lands, but then Edward I succeeded to the English throne and set out to gain control of the whole of Britain.

The Middle Ages and the last Welsh princes

Llywelyn gradually began to lose Welsh support and his brother Dafydd united against him with the ruler of Powys. Edward I seized his chance and the resulting struggle became known as the **First War of Welsh Independence** (1267-1277). The result was the **Treaty Of Aberconwy** (1277), in which Llywelyn lost most of his lands but was allowed to keep the title Prince of Wales. To keep the troublesome Welsh in order, Edward built castles at Flint, Aberystwyth, Builth Wells and Rhuddlan. A **Second War of Welsh Independence** was fought from 1282-1283, when Llywelyn's brother Dafydd rose against Edward, who brutally crushed the Welsh. Llywelyn was captured and killed at Cilmeri, near Builth Wells in 1282. Edward I strengthened his grip on Wales by starting to build more castles at Conwy, Caernarfon, Harlech and Beaumaris. In 1283 Dafydd was killed and the power of the Welsh princes ended.

In 1284 Edward signed the **Statute of Rhuddlan**, which established how Wales was to be governed; it was to be largely controlled by Norman lords and divided into new administrative units. English law took over for criminal matters, although Welsh law was retained for civil cases. Many of the powerful Welsh worked under this system happily enough and a rebellion in 1294 led by **Madog ap Llywelyn** was quickly crushed. In 1301 Edward revived the title of Prince of Wales, conferring it on his son Edward II, who had been born at Caernarfon.

The 14th century saw Britain plagued by famine and the Black Death, and Welsh anger and discontentment at their subjugation increased. The country was ripe for revolt – all

Arthur – the Once and Future King

With its ancient standing stones, prehistoric burial chambers, barren peaks and rich history it's not surprising that Wales is full of myths and legends, as well as tales of saints and holy wells, of giants and fairies, of Celtic gods and ghosts. And the best known figure of all is King Arthur.

The story of Arthur and the Knights of the Round Table is extraordinarily enduring and still inspires films and books. But did he exist? His name in Welsh, Arth Fawr, meaning the Great Bear, like the constellation Ursa Major, could point to him being a Celtic god. Some think the Arthurian legends date back to the Bronze Age, however, most sources feel he was probably a fifth-century Celtic chieftain who led the Brythonic Celts to victory against the Saxons. Though many places claim to be his birthplace, Tintagel in Cornwall seems the most likely, while Camelot could well be Cadbury Castle in Somerset. He is thought to have died at the battle of Camlan around AD539 and his burial place is generally agreed to be Glastonbury. Nothing very Welsh there then, yet Arthur has featured in Welsh folklore for centuries.

The first written references to him were made in the ninth-century *Historia Brittonum*, written by Nennius a monk from Bangor. Artorius was the 'dux bellorum' the leader who defeated the Saxons at Badon Hill in 518. By the 12th century he was a powerful symbol and was mentioned in the *Black Book of Carmarthen*, the oldest Welsh manuscript; in the *Mabinogion*, the famed collection of Welsh folk tales; and in Geoffrey of Monmouth's mammoth *Historia Regum Britanniae* – a 12-volume history of the kings of Britain. Geoffrey essentially wrote the first Arthurian romance and claimed that Caerleon, near Newport, was the site of his first court; the mound covering the ruined Roman amphitheatre there was known for years as Arthur's Round Table.

Later, writers embellished the myth, gradually turning Arthur from a Celtic leader to an idealized courtly knight. Chrétien de Troyes, a French poet, took the story to France and in the 15th century Sir Thomas Mallory wrote his influential *Morte d'Arthur*.

Welsh versions of his story abound, claiming that he fought his last battle on Snowdon; that Llyn Llydaw, a lake at the foot of Snowdon, was where the dying king was rowed out to the island of Avalon; that Excalibur was thrown by Sir Bedivere into Llyn Ogwen (or Llyn Llydaw or the lily pond at Bosherston…); and that Merlin sank the crown jewels into Llyn Cwmglas, a lake above the Llanberis Pass. Avalon is sometimes thought to be Bardsey Island; and Camlan, the site of his last battle, could be Cadlan on the Llyn Peninsula. Arthur, the Once and Future King, is still a powerful symbol of the Welsh struggle against oppression – a king who sleeps, waiting to come to the aid of the Celts once again.

they needed was a leader. In 1400, **Owain Glyndŵr** (1354-c1416) declared himself Prince of Wales and attacked ruling barons. He quickly gathered support and took castles such as Conwy, Harlech and Aberystwyth. Rebellion spread throughout Wales and Glyndŵr briefly established parliaments at Machynlleth and Dolgellau. He established alliances with powerful figures such as the Earl of Northumberland, and planned an independent Welsh state, garnering support from the Scots and the French. However, his support began to wane and after various defeats, with the Crown retaking Harlech and Aberystwyth castles he seemed to fade away. No one is sure how or when he died although it is thought to be 1416.

The Tudors

In 1485 Harri Tewdwr, a Welshman, took the English throne after winning the Battle of Bosworth with the help of a Welsh army. He became **Henry VII**, the first Tudor king, and Welsh hopes in him were high. He rewarded loyal Welsh nobles with high positions at court and sent letters to Welsh gentry in which he said he would restore 'the people... to their erst libertyes, delivering them of such miserable servitudes as they have pyteously longe stand in'. Restoration of 'libertyes' was not necessarily what Welsh nobles wanted – if interpreted in a certain way that could mean a return to the rigid traditional system of equal inheritance and the obstacles presented to the acquisition of land. They had seen at close hand the advantages of the English system of primogeniture and greater freedom in the transfer of land. The ruling class rapidly became anglicized.

Under Henry VIII's powerful administrator, Thomas Cromwell, Wales was brought far more under English control with the **Acts of Union** in 1536 and 1542. Although the Welsh were given legal equality, the legal system was unified with English common law taking the place of Welsh. The country was reorganized into shires, primogeniture became the method of inheritance and English became the language of the courts.

Elizabeth I

Under Elizabeth I, who wanted to ensure that Wales became Protestant rather than Catholic, an Act of Parliament was passed which laid down that the Bible be translated into Welsh within four years. This **Welsh Bible** should then be used in parishes where Welsh was the main language. The Welsh New Testament appeared in 1567, followed by the complete Bible in 1588. It was this that effectively saved the Welsh language. In 1547, the first Welsh book was published and, in 1571, Jesus College, Oxford was founded for Welsh scholars.

Civil War

During the Civil War, Wales was largely on the side of the King. Gradually Parliamentarian forces gained the upper hand but many castles resisted long sieges. **Harlech** was the last Royal castle to fall in 1647.

In 1752, Britain accepted the Gregorian Calendar. However, the Gwaun Valley in Pembrokeshire stayed with the Julian one – they still celebrate Julian New Year now.

Industrial Revolution

Wales was at the heart of the Industrial Revolution. While the north was rich in slate, the south was rich in iron ore, coal, limestone and water and the valleys around Merthyr Tydfil became huge centres for coal and iron production. Huge numbers of people migrated to the Valleys looking for work, and because many of them were not Welsh, local culture and language were weakened. The harsh conditions experienced by the workers gave rise to unrest throughout Britain. In Wales the **Merthyr Riots** of 1831 were particularly violent. The Red Flag was raised for the first time and many people, on both sides, were killed.

Insurrection continued with the **Chartist Riots**, the first of these in Wales took place in 1839 in Newport. The **Rebecca Riots** of 1839-1843 were a protest against toll gates on turnpike roads. They started on 13 May 1839 at Efail-wen. Rioters dressed in women's clothes and demolished the toll gates. The name was taken from a verse mentioning Rebecca in the Book of Genesis.

Welsh castles

The Welsh landscape is crammed with castles – brooding stone reminders of the country's turbulent history. There are 400 in all. But if you thought one was much like another you'd be wrong. Essentially there are three types of castle in Wales: those built by the Normans, those by the Welsh, and those by Edward I. They all have their own story to tell, and none more so than the handful of native Welsh castles that survive.

The first fortresses in Wales were erected by the Romans, whose imperial forces gradually subdued the ancient Britons who had retreated to this wild, western corner. However, castles, often built close to these Roman sites, did not appear until after the Norman Conquest and were erected by William's conquering forces to ensure that the locals knew just who was in charge. These were originally motte and bailey constructions of earth and timber, but later stone was used to create more robust structures. Most of the Norman castles in Wales are in the south and along the border with England. The first stone built castle in Britain was made by the Normans in Chepstow in 1067. It was the base for their aggressive incursions into Wales. Other Norman castles include Pembroke, Caerleon and Kidwelly.

In the 13th century, Welsh princes began to build their own castles, not just to provide protection against invading forces but also to guard against attacks from rival princes; this was a time when there were fierce internal struggles for control of Wales. These native Welsh castles were built in some of the most dramatic places in the country, utilising craggy outcrops and steep, isolated hills as natural defences. They tended to be smaller than Norman castles and often had a distinctive D-shaped tower. This had an outer, curved edge which gave a wide field of fire, and a flatter inner edge which meant that the rooms inside could be more spacious than in round towers. Only a few of these castles survive and they're often neglected by visitors. They include Castell-y-Bere, near Dolgellau, built to secure the southern border of Gwynedd; Dolbadarn, near Llanberis, and Dolwyddelan, south of Betws y Coed, which both guarded major routes through Snowdonia; and Dinefwr, in Carmarthenshire, which was the principal court of the kingdom of Deheubarth. Welsh castles fell into disrepair after the country was conquered by England, but the ruins are poignant and atmospheric reminders of the past.

The best known castles in Wales are those built by Edward I late in the 13th century. He was determined to complete the conquest of the Welsh, and as most danger came from North Wales, concentrated his building projects there. Some of his early castles were Rhuddlan and Conwy, and later Flint. But after Llywelyn the Last's second uprising he built even more enormous structures to create an iron ring of defence. These later castles of Harlech, Caernarfon, Conwy and finally Beaumaris remain among the most impressive and formidable castles in Europe. More information at www.castlewales.com.

Events such as the Rebecca Riots and the Chartist movement led many in authority to express concern at the increasingly negative attitude of the working classes. The issue of language, which was still being spoken in non-conformist schools, was thought to make the Welsh more prone to rioting. Welsh was also increasingly regarded as a handicap by parents, who saw it was important for their children to speak English so they could get on in industry and the professions. In 1846 a Welshman, representing an English constituency, set up an inquiry into Welsh education, focusing on the 'means afforded to the labouring classes of acquiring a knowledge of English'. English Anglicans were sent round the schools and came back with a report published in 1847. It declared that standards in education were terrible, which in many ways they were, but sadly they put much of this down to the use of Welsh. Their report was branded Brad y Llyfrau Gleision – the '**Treachery of the Blue Books**'. When free primary schools were set up in Wales in 1870, Welsh was largely banned. To dissuade pupils from speaking their language a 'Welsh Not' was introduced. This was a piece of wood on a strap which had to be worn, and was only passed on if someone else was heard speaking Welsh. The child left wearing the device would then be beaten.

In 1872 the system of education was expanded with the opening of the University College of Wales at Aberystwyth. A campaign began to grow for greater autonomy for Wales and there was a revival of interest in Welsh culture. The eisteddfod was reintroduced into Welsh life, the first being the National Eisteddfod of 1858. In 1885 the Welsh Language Society was created, which succeeded in ensuring that Welsh was taught in schools, and a political movement for a separate Wales was formed in 1886 as part of the Liberal party.

The political scene in Wales became increasingly radical and in 1900 Merthyr Tydfil elected a Scot, **Keir Hardie** as their MP – Britain's first Labour MP. The First World War saw a Welshman, **David Lloyd George** become prime minister. The Labour Party continued to grow in importance in Wales, but there was dissatisfaction at their failure to introduce home rule for Wales and the lack of safeguards for the language. In 1925 **Plaid Cymru**, the National Party of Wales was established. One of the founders was Saunder Lewis. He and two other Plaid members – DJ Williams and Lewis Valentine – gained notoriety (and Welsh support) when they set fire to buildings at an RAF station on the Llŷn.

After the Second World War, Labour came to power and a Welsh MP **Aneurin Bevan** established the National Health Service. Wales was still at the heart of the coal mining industry; the Valleys were tragically brought to the world's attention in October 1966 when a slag heap slid down a hill engulfing a school in the close-knit mining village of **Aberfan**:144 people were killed, 116 of whom were children.

Nationalism and devolution

Over the years, demands for home rule increased again and in 1979 a **referendum** was held. The result was huge disappointment for the nationalists with 80% of people voting against a Welsh assembly. But interest in the Welsh language did increase (the 1967 Welsh Language Act had already allowed the use of Welsh in court) and in 1982 a Welsh-language television channel, **S4C**, started up. Nationalist protests began to be directed at English 'incomers' – particularly at those buying second homes in Wales. The Sons of Glyndŵr started setting fire to English-owned holiday homes, giving rise to the joke 'Come home to a real fire – buy a Welsh cottage'.

After the Thatcher government was finally defeated and Labour took power again, another referendum was held in 1997. This time there was a tiny majority in favour and elections to the **National Assembly for Wales** took place in May 1999. Unlike the Scottish Parliament it has no tax-raising powers. After much wrangling work on a new building to house the assembly finally began in summer 2003. The Senedd, as it is known, was opened in 2006. It houses the National Assembly for Wales' Siambr (debating chamber) and Committee Rooms. The Assembly is made up of 60 Assembly Members – 40 representing individual constituencies and 20 representing the five regions of Wales. See www.assemblywales.org.

Culture

Literature

Myths and legends

The tradition of storytelling in Wales is rich and can be said to have its roots in the country's Celtic past. The Celts' religious system involved worship of gods, associated with natural features like flowers, trees and water. The Druids, the powerful religious and political Celtic leaders, had to undergo 20 years of training to acquire their sacred knowledge. This covered three areas: Druid – focusing on education and philosophy; Ovates – dealing with natural lore, divination and healing; and Bardic – the art of oratory – or powerful public speaking. Nothing was ever written down and everything had to be committed to memory. And with landscapes that inspire myths and legends (moody mountains, isolated islands, dank caves, ancient burial sites) there was plenty of material to inspire the early storytellers. And the battles fought both on and for the land, the arrival of the early Christian saints, and the colourful characters in Welsh history all added to this inspirational cocktail.

Many of the earliest stories survive in the *Mabinogion*, a rich collection of Welsh mythical tales written down around the 13th and 14th centuries but of much earlier origin. The *Mabinogion* were eventually translated into English in the 19th century by Lady Charlotte Guest, who gave them their collective title, which means '*Tales of Youth*'. Characters who feature include Blodeuwedd, a girl who was created from flowers; and Culhwch, who has to perform forty feats to win the hand of Olwen, daughter of a local giant. He pulls it off with the help of King Arthur and his knights.

The Arthurian legends are rich in Wales. Not only do they appear in the Mabinogion but are also mentioned in the ninth century Historia Brittonum, a Latin history of Britain by Nennius who, according to what you read, was either a monk in Wales or a military leader from Scotland. Arthur is considered by many to have been a tribal leader who, much like Boudicca, fought off Saxon invaders. Merlin the magician, of the legends, is also said to be Welsh – probably a sixth-century holy man called Myrddin who was born near Carmarthen. Whether fact or fiction, Arthur certainly featured in an early Welsh poem, *Y Gododdin*; written around the seventh century by the bard Aneurin, it describes a battle against the Saxons.

Travel writing

Travel writers have also been intrigued by Wales' unique combination of ancient language, rich history and stunning scenery. The first was **Giraldus Cambrensis**, or Gerald of Wales, who was born at Manorbier in 1146. Of Norman descent, he travelled widely through Wales trying to drum up recruits to go on the Third Crusade, and wrote detailed accounts of his travels. The books, *The Journey Through Wales* and *The Description of Wales*, give a vivid insight into Welsh life and people in the 12th century. Other travel books include **Thomas Pennant's** A Tour in Wales (1773), which ushered in a passion for wild and romantic Welsh landscapes; **HV Morton's** In Search of Wales; and **George Borrow's** still widely quoted *Wild Wales* (1854). Borrow was English but had learned Welsh and reported his conversations in detail. He is often seen as typifying English condescending attitudes towards the Welsh – but as this is the man who wrote "an Englishman of the lower class ... is never savage with you, provided you call him old chap, and he considers you by your dress to be his superior in station" he was obviously happy to patronize anyone, not just the Welsh.

Poetry

Poetry has enormous importance in Wales, with Aneurin and Taliesin – a sixth-century bard associated with the poems that appeared in the 14th-century *Book of Taliesin* – providing the earliest examples of Welsh poetry. Poets were important members of the royal courts and Welsh princes had their own poets to record battles and important events – and praise their bosses, a bit like the Poet Laureate today. The earliest known of these professional bards was a man named Meilyr who lived in the 12th century. An intricate and characteristic form of poetry writing gradually developed at these courts. Known as *cynghanedd* – the use of vivid imagery and elaborate patterns of rhyme and alliteration – its influence can still be seen today.

Poetry was considered so important that competitions were established, with poets competing for privileged positions. The first recorded large scale competition – or eisteddfod – took place in 1176 at Rhys ap Gruffydd's castle in Cardigan. These flourished until the 17th and 18th centuries, when they began to peter out, until they were revived in the 19th century. Poetry had enormous significance for the Welsh, often mourning the loss of great leaders who had fought their English/Norman rulers, and stirring the emotions of a people who desperately wanted to be free.

19th- and 20th-century literature

After 1870 the speaking of English, rather than Welsh, was enforced in schools and a new Anglo/Welsh literature emerged, with Welsh people writing in English but being influenced by the Welsh writing traditions and patterns of speech. The country itself also acted as inspiration to poets. The Jesuit poet **Gerard Manley Hopkins** (1844-1889), writing in the 1870s and 1880s, was inspired and moved by the Welsh countryside as well as the rhythm of the language. And **Edward Thomas** (1878-1917) who was of Welsh extraction, produced fine poems inspired by nature until he was killed at the Front in the First World War. **WH Davies** (1871-1940), a friend of Thomas, left Wales for America, where his experiences on the road inspired the once bestselling, but now less widely read, *Autobiography of a Super-Tramp*. However his lines "What is this life if, full of care/We have no time to stand and stare" have entered the British lexicon.

The 20th century saw the real flowering of Welsh writing – and not only were Welsh people writing in English, Wales itself was inspiring literature. **Caradoc Evans** (1914-1945) wrote controversial and satirical works about non-conformist Wales; novelist **Richard Hughes** (1900-1976), author of *High Wind in Jamaica*, lived and worked in Laugharne; **Alexander Cordell** (1914-1997) settled in Wales and wrote novels inspired by Welsh historical events such as the Rebecca Riots; **Kingsley Amis** (1922-1995) lectured at Swansea University – the setting for his novel *Lucky Jim* (1954), and Welshman **Alun Lewis** (1915-1944) produced some of the most important poetry of the Second World War. The book that really grabbed popular attention was **Richard Llewellyn**'s *How Green Was My Valley* (1939), a worldwide bestseller depicting life in the coalfields of south Wales – which later got the Hollywood treatment in a film.

The most acclaimed 20th-century writers were poets RS Thomas and Dylan Thomas. **RS Thomas** (1913-2000) was a clergyman and prolific writer who was inspired by the landscapes and history of Wales. His work had a bleak quality "There is no present in Wales/ And no future;/ There is only the past." He was a fierce nationalist too and spoke out on issues such as the spread of the English language into isolated, mainly Welsh-speaking areas. **Dylan Thomas** (1914-1953) is the best known of all Welsh writers, not only because of the high quality of his rich, original and lyrical verse, but also because of his reputation for hard living and hard drinking. Born in Swansea, his first volume of work was *Eighteen Poems* which was received to widespread acclaim. Over the years he moved to London and then back to Wales, producing fine poems with instantly recognizable lines such as: "Do not go gentle into that good night" and "The force that through the green fuse". He also wrote the dense and compelling *Under Milk Wood*, his 'play for voices', which produced characters such as Captain Cat and Polly Garter. When he wasn't writing poetry he was investigating the pubs of southwest Wales. His heavy drinking leading to his untimely death in America, where a particularly hard session resulted in "an insult to the brain".

Literature today

Literature is flourishing in Wales today and it is worth looking for works by poets such as **Menna Elfyn**, **Owen Sheers** and **Harri Webb**; Welsh romantic novels by the prolific **Iris Gower**, and works by **Kate Roberts** set in the quarries of north Wales. Then there's the Welsh Irvine Welsh, **Niall Griffiths**, whose books like *Grits* and *Sheepshagger* look at the seamy side of contemporary life; **James Hawes**, whose *White Powder, Green Light*, focuses on the Welsh media; and **Malcolm Pryce's** blackly comic *Aberystwyth Mon Amour*.

Music

Wales and Music – a musical tradition

The epithet 'land of song' has been attached to Wales since Adam was a lad. And, true enough, the country has a powerful musical tradition. Its male voice choirs are known throughout the world, and top-flight artists such as Tom Jones and Shirley Bassey are household names. The Welsh National Opera has performed in the world's foremost venues. When virtuoso Bryn Terfel appeared at the Metropolitan Opera in 1998, he made the front page of the *New York Times*, and hot mezzo soprano Katherine Jenkins has a huge following. But these are conventional examples of the nation's culture – there's a lot more in the musical melting pot than this. Wales has an eclectic attitude to music, revelling in its many facets. Organizations such as Cultural Concerns bring musicians from around the globe: Burundi, Iran, Zimbabwe, India, Poland, Colombia to name a few, to perform in Wales. Likewise, Welsh artists take the opportunity to explore cultural differences and indeed similarities, in far-flung corners of the globe. And as for rock and pop, Wales produced The Manic Street Preachers, Stereophonics, Catatonia, Feeder, Super Furry Animals and Gorky's Zygotic Mynci, a pretty illustrious track record if ever there was one.

But why Wales and song? Why do the lusty voices of the rugby crowd belt out 'Calon Lan' and 'Sosban Fach' while the match is in full flood? What drives thousands of people to a free concert given by Welsh National Opera in Cardiff Bay? Why do pubs throughout the land reverberate to the sound, not only of the jukebox, but of imbibers boisterously accompanying their favourite number? And this isn't just drunken crooning, it actually sounds melodic!

Music, and song, is, and always has been, a compelling form of self-expression. Furthermore, Celtic societies, be they Breton, Cornish, Irish, Scottish or Welsh, have always cherished music. Music affirms an individual's sense of place and belonging. Traditional Welsh music explores the universal themes of love and desire, but it also explores the condition of *hiraeth*. No single word sums up this emotion, a sense of loss and longing and nostalgia. Expats express a sense of *hiraeth* when they think of home. But *hiraeth* is more than homesickness, it's part of the human condition, an inexpressible yearning. Inexpressible, that is, other than through music and song. Although the Welsh do a fine line in poetry and prose, the voice of the nation is most eloquently and profoundly expressed through the medium of music.

The earliest recorded instrument in Wales is the **crwth**, or lyre. There's evidence to suggest that it was played as far back as Roman times. This rudimentary instrument wasn't peculiar to the Celts though. An illustration on an Egyptian tomb circa 1900 BC shows a musician holding a six-stringed instrument that is, to all intents and purposes, a crwth. Its heyday came in the Middle Ages when players made a good living entertaining the Welsh aristocracy. Its popularity declined with the advent of the fiddle, with its infinitely more dexterous repertoire. Now, originals can be found at the Museum of Welsh Life in St Fagan's near Cardiff and in the National Library of Wales in Aberystwyth. However, the age of the crwth isn't completely over. Enthusiasts, such as widely acclaimed fiddle player Cass Meurig, still perform traditional crwth music and replicas are lovingly fashioned by Cardiff-based craftsman, Guy Flockhart.

Bagpipes may be synonymous with Scotland, but all Celtic nations have their own version. The Welsh manifestation is called the 'piba cwd'. Popular until the latter half of the nineteenth century, it is extraordinary that no examples have survived to the present day. Another popular instrument was the **pibgorn**, literally meaning hornpipe, which was not unique to Wales. This simple instrument is powered by a single reed like the drone reed of a bagpipe.

The **triple harp**, with its sweetly lyrical sound, is another instrument closely aligned with Wales. Unlike the crwth it has a prominent place in today's culture. Prince Charles revived an ancient tradition when he appointed 20-year-old Catrin Finch as Royal Harpist. The young Welshwoman's mission is to bring the harp to the masses. With her youth and good looks, she has a better chance of success than most of making the harp hip.

The Welsh **male voice choir** (cor meibion) is something of an institution. Although male choirs are found throughout the nation, they are perhaps most closely associated with the mining communities in South Wales. The demise of the coal industry isn't reflected in the fate of the choirs, joining one might not be a funky move, but the tradition still holds firm.

Classical music enjoys a high profile in Wales. Cardiff hosts the acclaimed *Singer of the World* competition, attended by the great and the good among classical vocalists, on an annual basis. **Welsh National Opera** (WNO) is recognized as one of the UK's finest companies, and was the first ever regional company to appear at Covent Garden. The performing arts are devotedly nurtured at the Welsh College of Music and Drama and within the BBC's National Orchestra of Wales.

The **Manic Street Preachers** paved the way for Wales to become a feature on the rock'n'roll map. Catatonia's **Cerys Matthews**, raunchy and vivid, coined the immortal words 'Everyday I wake up, and thank the lord I'm Welsh.' For a brief and wonderful moment, the South Wales city Newport was hailed as the new Seattle. For those jaded with the 'We'll Keep A Welcome in the Hillsides' image of Wales, this feisty new face represented a freedom from the shackles of tradition. For the first time ever it was cool to be Welsh. The term 'Cool Cymru' or 'Cool Wales' entered the lexicon.

Rhondda, the most famous of all the South Wales mining valleys, struck out into new waters with a musical venture called **The Factory** (formerly The Pop Factory) ⓣ *T02920-230130, www.factoryporth.com*. This sleek venue and television complex has worked hard to attract big names, with notable success.

Despite the success of Welsh bands, some would say that the contemporary music scene has stalled. At least, in terms of bands big enough to hit the headlines and stay there. However, all is not lost. The Welsh Music Foundation has been set up to nurture modern Welsh music, and maximize its cultural and economic potential. Sadly, to date, the mother country has benefited very little in monetary terms from the success of its high-flying sons and daughters. In future that should change, and Wales can reap financial and emotional rewards from her aeons-long love affair with music.

Welsh language

Welsh origins

Welsh is an Indo-European language presumably descended like many languages in modern Western Europe from languages that were originally spoken on the steppes of Central Asia. It is immediately descended from the Brythonic language, its closest relatives are other Celtic languages – Cornish and Breton. To the present day there remain differences in dialects throughout Wales, the most notable being: Y Wyndodeg (northwest), Y Buwyseg (northeast and mid Wales), Y Ddyfydeg (southwest), Gwenhwyseg (southeast).

During the dark ages, Wales was ruled by a number of different Welsh dynastic principalities who from time to time made alliances with each other and English rulers. It was during this time that the Brythonic language was consolidated and became widespread throughout Wales. It was influenced to a degree by the Roman occupation, and even today, the Welsh language shows Latin influences with words like *pont* (bridge), *ffenestre* (window), *caws* (cheese) and *cwmwl* (cloud).

In the 15th century, Wales was absorbed into the English state under Henry VIII. This was the first reference to the Welsh language. The passing of the 1536 and 1542 Acts of Union brought significant change as it stated that English should be the only language in courts. Use of the Welsh language, in an official capacity, was not lawful again until the passing of the Welsh Courts Act in 1942.

On the request of Elizabeth I, the Bible was translated by William Morgan in 1588, establishing a nationwide standard for the language. Welsh was permitted as the language of religion and church, helping to safeguard it. Had this not been the case the language could have disappeared completely at this stage.

In 1847, the 'Report of the Commissioners of Inquiry Into the State of Education in Wales', written by three English commissioners, emphasized the superiority of the English language. The 'Welsh not' or 'Welsh stick' was introduced in some schools – a form of punishment handed out to pupils found speaking Welsh, which could result in a beating. This practice became a symbol of oppression of the language.

The establishment of 'Yr Eisteddfod Genedlaethol' in the 19th century and the importance of the Welsh chapel, frequently the centre of Welsh life, were important in keeping the grass-roots language alive. By 1911, nearly a million people regarded themselves as Welsh speakers. However, social change such as urbanization, industrialization and the secularization of society, led to English becoming the main language (50%) in some areas.

National Eisteddfod

The National Eisteddfod, an annual cultural festival and competition to celebrate Welsh culture, is now a vital part of the Welsh calendar. In 1938, a petition was launched at the Eisteddfod calling for a repeal of the Act of Union, demanding that Welsh be given equal status with English. The petition, signed by more than a quarter of a million people and supported by a number of Welsh MPs, led to the Welsh Courts Act of 1942. The Welsh language became legally acceptable in schools, for academic studies and the media; however, the language clause of the Act of Union remained, which held sway in the courts of law.

Welsh National Party

Plaid Genedlaethol Cymru (The Welsh National Party) was formed in Pwllheli in 1925 by a small group of intellectuals and their leader, Saunders Lewis, focused the party efforts on the defence of the Welsh language. Cymdeithas yr Iaith was established in 1962 as one of the first single issue pressure groups. Using a non-violent means of civil disobedience, it led a campaign towards the Welsh Language Act 1967, which made the existence of Welsh language a more accepted part of life in the principality. It is predominately due to Cymdeithas yr Iaith that you will see bilingual road signs, as this was brought about in the 1960s when they launched a large-scale campaign against monolingual road signs.

The activities of Cymdeithas yr Iaith coincided with the granting to Wales of a significant degree of administrative autonomy by the appointment of a Minister of State for Wales in 1964 and the establishment of the Welsh Office.

Education and media

In 1988 the Education Reform Act ensured that all children aged between 5-16 would be taught Welsh as a core subject in Welsh medium schools. The growth in Welsh-medium education in places such as Cardiff produced considerable numbers of Welsh speakers and helped vary the social base of the language. The growth of Welsh in Anglicized districts was particularly evident in the results of the 1991 census.

Sianel Pedwar Cymru (S4C– Welsh Channel Four) was first broadcast in November 1982. This channel produces Welsh language programmes with English subtitles and a number of S4C's programmes are viewed across Europe. In the early 1980s when other sectors of the Welsh economy were in decline, there was significant rise in employment in Welsh language television. Welsh, in all aspects of life, has been given a higher status, particularly since the launch of the 1993 Welsh Language Act.

Devolution

In 1997 the devolution referendum was seen as an opportunity for greater autonomy for Wales and was supported as a means to reassert the 'Welsh' identity. The economic benefits of the Welsh language are being recognized, leading to the ability to communicate in Welsh and English in the workplace being recognized as a valuable skill and marketable commodity. The 2001 census identified the first increase in number and percentage of Welsh speakers in 20 counties, with the southeast showing the greatest rise. The language is evolving and gradually English phrases are being absorbed into the Welsh language.

Despite the turbulent times the language has experienced, its increased usage in all sectors of Welsh society has ensured a place in the hearts of the growing proportion of the population who chose to learn or pass on knowledge of the language. Welsh, one of the oldest European languages, is now spoken by almost a quarter of the population of Wales and a visitor is sure to see unusual phrases and hear unfamiliar sounds, but this is part of Wales' charm. Try and get your tongue around some basic 'Welsh' and you'll receive a warm welcome wherever you go.

Books

Fiction

Brito, Leonora, *Dat's Love* (1995), Seren Books. Story of the ethnic community in Cardiff Bay.

Cordell, Alexander, *Rape of the Fair Country* (2000), *Song of the Earth* (1999), *Hosts of Rebecca* (1998), Blorenge. This popular trilogy is set in the area around the Blaenavon ironworks during the time leading up to the Rebecca Riots.

Evans, Richard John, *Entertainment* (2000), Seren. Lively account of living in the Rhonnda Valley.

Gower, Iris, *Copper Kingdom* (1984), *Black Gold* (1989), Arrow. Two of a number of books written by one of Wales' best-known romantic novelists.

Griffiths, Niall, *Sheepshagger* (2002), *Grits* (2001), *Kelly & Victor* (2002), *Stump* (2004), Vintage. A sort of Welsh Irvine Welsh, dealing with drugs and the seamy side of life in Wales.

Hawes, James, *White Powder, Green Light* (2003), Jonathan Cape. A sly look at the media industry in Wales.

Jones, Dave and **Rivers, Tony**, *The Soul Crew* (2002), Milo Books. Looking at the sub- culture of football hooligans who follow Cardiff FC.

Llewellyn, Richard, *How Green Was My Valley*. (2001), Penguin. Probably the best known of all books about life in the Valleys.

Pryce, Malcolm, *Aberystwyth Mon Amour*. (2002), Bloomsbury. Black comedy set in contemporary Aberystwyth. Also *Last Tango in Aberystwyth* (2004), *The Unbearable Lightness of Being in Aberystwyth* (2005), *From Aberystwyth with Love* (2010) and *The Day Aberystwyth Stood Still* (2012).

Travel writing

Abley, Mark, *Spoken Here* (2004), Heinemann. Account of the author's travels in countries that have threatened languages – or ones that are fighting back. Includes a chapter on Wales.

Borrow, George, *Wild Wales* (1955), Gomer Press. Classic account of a 19th-century walking tour of Wales by pompous, Welsh-speaking Englishman.

Morris, Jan, *Wales* (2000), Penguin. Rich and informative insight into the country written by Anglo-Welsh travel writer.

Morton, HV, *In Search of Wales* (1986), Methuen. Written when the scholarly author travelled Wales in the 1930s.

Rogers, Byron, *The Bank Manager and the Holy Grail* (Aurum 2003). Travels into the eccentric side of Wales.

Sager, Peter, *Wales* (2002), Pallas. Extremely readable account of the country, its history and its culture.

Poetry

Lycett, Andrew, *Dylan Thomas a New Life* (2004), Weidenfeld and Nicolson. A biography of the poet.

Manley Hopkins, Gerard, *Collected Works*, Penguin. The Jesuit poet was much influenced by the landscape of Wales.

Sheers, Owen, *The Blue Book* (Seren 2000) and *Skirrid Hill* (2005). Poetry from Wales' award-winning poet.

Thomas, Dylan, *The Dylan Thomas Omnibus* (1999), Phoenix. An accessible collection of the poet's works.

Thomas, RS, *Selected Poems* (2000), Phoenix. Poetry of the fiery, nationalist priest.

Webb, Harri, *Collected Poems* (1995), Gomer Press. More contemporary poetry.

Footnotes

Contents

Useful words and phrases

Alphabet (Yr Wyddor)
a, b, c, ch, d, dd, e, f, ff, g, ng, h, i, i, l, ll, m, n, o, p, ph, r, rh, s, t, th, u, w, y

Vowels (llafariad)
a, e, i, o, u, w, y

A aah	B bee	C eck	CH ech
D dee	DD edd	E air	F ev
FF eff	G egg	NG eng	H high-tsh
I ee	J jay	L el	LL ell
M em	N en	O oh	P pee
PH phee	R air	RH air-hee	S ess
T tee	TH eth	U ee	W oo Y uh

Welsh place names	**Meaning**	**Pronunciation**
Abertawe (Swansea)	Estuary	Ab-er-taw-eh
Beddgelert	Grave	Be-the-gel-airt
Betws-y-**Coed**	Wood	Bet-oos uh koyd
Caerdydd (Cardiff)	Fort	K-ie-r-dee-the
Cas**newydd**(Newport)	New	Kas ne with
Dinbych-y-**Pysgod** (Denbigh)	Fish	Din-bich uh pusg-od
Glan **Llyn**	Lake	Glan ll-in
Llandeilo	Church	ll-an-day-lo
Sir Benfro (Pembrokeshire)	County	Seer Ben Vr-aw
Y **Dre**newydd (Newtown)	Town	Uh Drair ne with
Ynys Mon (Anglesey)	Island	Un- is Morn

Llanfairpwllgwyngyllgogerychwyrndrobwllllantysiliogogogoch

Roughly translated as:
The Church of St Mary by the pool with the white hazel near the rapid whirlpool by St Tysilio's church and the red cave.

Have a go at pronouncing it:
Thlann vyre pooth gwin gith gogger ich chweern drobbooth lann tuss-illyo goggo gauch.

Other useful phrases:

Bore Da	good morning	*Prynhawn da*	good afternoon
Nos da	good night	*Hwyl fawr*	good bye
Diolch	thank you	*Dim diolch*	no thank you
Os gwelwch chi'n dda	please	*Faint?*	how much?
Gwely a brecwast	bed and breakfast	*Lwc dda*	Good luck
Paned o de	cup of tea	*Paned o goffi*	cup of coffee

Glossary

A

Afon – river
Amgueddfa – museum
Ap (ab) – son of
Ar Agor – open
Ar Gau – closed

B

Bach – small
Bara – bread
Blaen – head of valley
Brenhines – queen
Brenin – king
Bryn – hill
Bwlch – pass
Brecwast – breakfast
Bws – bus

C

Cadair – chair, stronghold
Capel – chapel
Carn – rock, mountain
Carreg – rock, stone
Castell – castle
Cefn – ridge
Clun – meadow
Coch – red
Croeso – welcome
Cwm – valley (or combe)
Cymraeg – Welsh
Cymru – Wales
Cymry – the Welsh people

D

Da – good
Ddu / Du – black
De – south
Dinas – town, fort
Dŵr – water
Dwyrain – east
Dydd – day

E

Eglwys – church

F

Fawr – big
Fferm – farm
Ffordd – road, way
Fforest – forest
Ffynnon – well

G

Glan – river bank
Gardd – garden
Glas – blue
Glyn – vallley, glen
Gogledd – north
Gorllewin – west
Gorsaf – station
Gwely – bed
Gwesty – hotel
Gwyn – white
Gwyrdd – green

H

Hafod – summer dwelling for herdsmen
Heddiw – today
Hen – old
Heol – road
Hiraeth – yearning

I

Isaf – lower

L

Llechen – slate
Llety – lodging
Llwybr – path
Llys – court

M

Maen – rock, stone
Maes – field
Mawr – big, great
Melin – mill
Melyn – yellow
Merthyr – martyr
Môr – sea
Morfa – marsh
Mynydd – mountain

N

Nant – stream
Neuadd – hall
Newydd – new
Nos – night

O

Ogof – cave

P

Pant – dip
Parc – park
Pen – head of
Pentre/pentref – village
Plas – hall (large house)
Pont (bont) – bridge
Porth – port or doorway

R

Rhaeadr – waterfall
Rhiw – hill

S

Saesneg – English (language)
Sarn – causeway
Sant – saint
Siop – shop
Stryd – street
Swyddfa'r Post – post office

T

Tafarn – pub
Theatr – theatre
Traeth – beach
Tre, tref – town
Tŵr – tower
Tŷ – house

U

Uchaf – highest

Y

Y, Yr, 'r' – the
Yn – in
Ysbyty – hospital
Ysgol – school

Index

Titles available in the Footprint *Focus* range

Latin America	UK RRP	US RRP
Bahia & Salvador	£7.99	$11.95
Brazilian Amazon	£7.99	$11.95
Brazilian Pantanal	£6.99	$9.95
Buenos Aires & Pampas	£7.99	$11.95
Cartagena & Caribbean Coast	£7.99	$11.95
Costa Rica	£8.99	$12.95
Cuzco, La Paz & Lake Titicaca	£8.99	$12.95
El Salvador	£5.99	$8.95
Guadalajara & Pacific Coast	£6.99	$9.95
Guatemala	£8.99	$12.95
Guyana, Guyane & Suriname	£5.99	$8.95
Havana	£6.99	$9.95
Honduras	£7.99	$11.95
Nicaragua	£7.99	$11.95
Northeast Argentina & Uruguay	£8.99	$12.95
Paraguay	£5.99	$8.95
Quito & Galápagos Islands	£7.99	$11.95
Recife & Northeast Brazil	£7.99	$11.95
Rio de Janeiro	£8.99	$12.95
São Paulo	£5.99	$8.95
Uruguay	£6.99	$9.95
Venezuela	£8.99	$12.95
Yucatán Peninsula	£6.99	$9.95

Asia	UK RRP	US RRP
Angkor Wat	£5.99	$8.95
Bali & Lombok	£8.99	$12.95
Chennai & Tamil Nadu	£8.99	$12.95
Chiang Mai & Northern Thailand	£7.99	$11.95
Goa	£6.99	$9.95
Gulf of Thailand	£8.99	$12.95
Hanoi & Northern Vietnam	£8.99	$12.95
Ho Chi Minh City & Mekong Delta	£7.99	$11.95
Java	£7.99	$11.95
Kerala	£7.99	$11.95
Kolkata & West Bengal	£5.99	$8.95
Mumbai & Gujarat	£8.99	$12.95

For the latest books, e-books and a wealth of travel information, visit us at: www.footprinttravelguides.com.

Africa & Middle East	UK RRP	US RRP
Beirut	£6.99	$9.95
Cairo & Nile Delta	£8.99	$12.95
Damascus	£5.99	$8.95
Durban & KwaZulu Natal	£8.99	$12.95
Fès & Northern Morocco	£8.99	$12.95
Jerusalem	£8.99	$12.95
Johannesburg & Kruger National Park	£7.99	$11.95
Kenya's Beaches	£8.99	$12.95
Kilimanjaro & Northern Tanzania	£8.99	$12.95
Luxor to Aswan	£8.99	$12.95
Nairobi & Rift Valley	£7.99	$11.95
Red Sea & Sinai	£7.99	$11.95
Zanzibar & Pemba	£7.99	$11.95

Europe	UK RRP	US RRP
Bilbao & Basque Region	£6.99	$9.95
Brittany West Coast	£7.99	$11.95
Cádiz & Costa de la Luz	£6.99	$9.95
Granada & Sierra Nevada	£6.99	$9.95
Languedoc: Carcassonne to Montpellier	£7.99	$11.95
Málaga	£5.99	$8.95
Marseille & Western Provence	£7.99	$11.95
Orkney & Shetland Islands	£5.99	$8.95
Santander & Picos de Europa	£7.99	$11.95
Sardinia: Alghero & the North	£7.99	$11.95
Sardinia: Cagliari & the South	£7.99	$11.95
Seville	£5.99	$8.95
Sicily: Palermo & the Northwest	£7.99	$11.95
Sicily: Catania & the Southeast	£7.99	$11.95
Siena & Southern Tuscany	£7.99	$11.95
Sorrento, Capri & Amalfi Coast	£6.99	$9.95
Skye & Outer Hebrides	£6.99	$9.95
Verona & Lake Garda	£7.99	$11.95

North America	UK RRP	US RRP
Vancouver & Rockies	£8.99	$12.95

Australasia	UK RRP	US RRP
Brisbane & Queensland	£8.99	$12.95
Perth	£7.99	$11.95

Join us on facebook for the latest travel news, product releases, offers and amazing competitions: www.facebook.com/footprintbooks.